You're Never Too Old to Dream Dare Dance!

For every woman over 40

Jan Fraser

Jan Fraser

Sally Huss

Lila Larson

Joanne Proctor

Sue Savage

www.dreamdaredance.com

BERMUDA MEDIA
HAMILTON, BERMUDA
Copyright 2009 @ Bermuda Media

YOU'RE NEVER TOO OLD TO DREAM DARE DANCE!
Cover Design and Musings by Sally Huss
Manuscript Edited by Kathrine Kramer
Text Design by Casey Hooper
Back Cover Photo Design by Colin Hassell

Printed in the U.S.A.

Contributors listed in the *Dream Dare Dance With Us!* Chapter

To order this title, please visit www.dreamdaredance.com or contact:
Bermuda Media
26 Bermudiana Road
P.O. Box HM2032
Hamilton HM HX
Bermuda
submit@bm.bm

Library of Congress Cataloging-in-Publication Data available upon request.
ISBN 978-0-9801104-1-8

This book is dedicated to Marlene Coleman, M.D., wife, mother, sister, author, teacher, speaker, pediatrician, U.S. Navy captain, philanthropist, coach, medical board member, armchair psychologist, and dear friend.

Marlene quietly passed away on January 26, 2009, with her twin sister, Darlene, by her side. Bill, her loving husband of 25 years, passed away on November 26, 2008, five days after hearing Marlene's doctor give her two months to live. (I believe their love was perfect and he didn't want to be on this earth without her.)

On April 26, 2008, Marlene gave me a book called *Always Follow Your Dreams*, which contained a poem by Vicki Silvers. It is an uplifting, you-can-do-anything-you-set-your-mind-to book. I read it every night before I go to sleep. It is a perfect Marlene book. This is one of my favorite passages:

> Keep your belief
> In yourself
> And walk into your new journey.
>
> You will find it magnificent,
> Spectacular,
> And beyond your wildest
> Imaginings.

I am picturing Marlene in a whole new world where she has thousands who love and appreciate her just as we treasure her here—a magnificent world beyond her wildest imaginings. Thank you, Vicki Silvers, for putting words to my dreams for our Marlene.

Marlene was a continual support for our Dream Dare Dance! book and we are grateful.

Let's dance in Marlene's memory. Let's use Marlene's example of love and support by gifting a copy of this book to each of our friends who may need inspiration to live their dreams. Encourage them with a fitting inscription like the one Marlene wrote to me: "Bravo! Go Girl Go! You're really doin' it!"

Jan Fraser
July 2009

Contents

Part One – Dream

Part Two – Dare

Part Three – Dance

Foreword

*D*reams really do come true.

In my law of attraction work, I know how powerful dreams can be to the success and fulfillment of life's joys. I am continually recommending dream work to my trainers and my speaking audiences. I know that what we focus on becomes reality.

When I was approached to write the foreword for *You're Never Too Old to Dream Dare Dance!*, it appealed to me for several reasons.

One, I believe in the purpose and need to create more dreaming in our world. Over the last 40 years as a motivational speaker, I have emphasized the need to keep one's dreams and goals in sight because they are more likely to manifest themselves if we do.

Two, I work with the five women who are at the heart of this book and know the magic they create in the lives of others. They are speakers, trainers, coaches, counselors, and mentors. The insights and wisdom they offer in this book will inspire countless women.

Third, the stories are true. My *Chicken Soup for the Soul®* stories are read around the world, bringing hope, courage, inspiration, and love to millions of people. Sharing our stories of hope, triumph, and resiliency is an unquestionably powerful tool in transforming people's lives. I hope you will allow the stories in this book to change your life.

You're Never Too Old to Dream Dare Dance! is a feast for women over 40 who may have put their dreams on the back burner, lost sight of their dreams, or need brand new ones. This insightful book will no doubt help you to face life's challenges as you find and realize your dreams.

I not only bought this book for my wife, I have recommended it to her friends and all the women on my mailing list. It is a must read for any woman who wants to be feel happy, joyous, and free to make her dreams come true.

Jack Canfield
Co-Founder, *Chicken Soup for the Soul® best-selling series*

Preface

*D*ream Dare Dance! is about dusting off dreams and creating new ones. We are encouraging every woman who reads this book to go for her dreams. Seize this moment in time. Choose to create more love, joy, passion, and success in her life.

Whether your dream is to find a job, write a book, fall in love, be happy, improve your health, launch a new career, eradicate malaria, or run 200 miles over three countries in eight days, we hope you will gather courage, strength, and love in the pages of this book to find and fulfill your personal dream.

In this book, you will read the stories of many courageous women who have achieved their dreams through unsinkable spirit. By sharing their stories and our insights, we hope to inspire you to dream, dare you to take action, and dance to celebrate your achievement. *Dream Dare Dance!*

We invite you to join us on this dream path.

We believe your dreams will come true.

With Love,
Jan Fraser, Sally Huss, Lila Larson,
Joanne Proctor, and Sue Savage

Acknowledgements

A grateful thank you to all of the wonderful people who gave their time and truth to review the first draft of our manuscript. We appreciate you for helping us make our dream come true and, in turn, helping other women do the same.

Karen Axline

Liz Buchanan

Pat Christianson

Burdie L. Dixon

Sherri Dolleman

Patricia Duthoit

Anne Felton

Karen Gridley

Peggy Hormberg

Bill Huggins

Kathleen Hurley

Cathy Vernon-Irving

Dawn Krawczyk

Linda Landis

Bonnie Leviss

Lois Lussier

LaRae Matteo

Lynn MAcMartin

Joanne McBean

Bernie Pignatello

Sylvia Relitz

Donna Rogers

Margaret Sansom

Mary Shaver

Leone Stacheruk

Jude Wilcox

Eileen Wood

Introduction

*M*idlife—who me? How'd that happen? Midlife surprises many women. It's a term that can make your skin crawl. Suddenly, it seems, we find ourselves just a little bit older and with a little less time ahead of us. With advances in health care, we are blessed with the possibility that we may live 40, 50, 60, even 70-plus years after turning 40.

Questions arise: Who am I? Where am I going? What do I want the second half of my life to look like?

We believe that the second half of life can be the best time of our lives. We believe midlife can be a time of great joy. "Midjoy," we like to call it.

The middle years offer an amazing opportunity—the opportunity to find and act on what matters to you most. We believe it really is possible to create the life of your dreams, whatever that may be for you. It may involve finding a life purpose, changing a relationship, filling your empty nest, enjoying good health, facing difficult emotional or health-related issues, or finding a way to juggle all the moving parts of your life. The possibilities are endless.

This book is intended to inspire and help you to take steps toward living the life you want, whatever you know or discover that to be. We hope to inspire you to *dream, dare, and dance.*

We are encouraging you to *dream*—to imagine what has yet to be, to open yourself to new possibilities within yourself and for your life, to discover what it is you desire, to travel to places in your mind you haven't thought about for a long time, have put on hold, or never even imagined.

We are encouraging you to *dare*—to face the challenges in midlife and to take the steps necessary to realize your dreams.

We are encouraging you to *dance*—to celebrate your accomplishments and experience the joy of traveling the path to your dreams.

This is what it means to *Dream Dare Dance!*

Dream Dare Dance! is full of the voices of women from all walks of life who share their stories here so that you too will be inspired to face what is before you and to create the life you want. We hope these stories—and our insights—will inspire you and give you the courage to go after your dreams. Seize this moment in time. Choose to create more love, joy, passion, and success in your life.

Take this journey of discovery with us. You too can discover the joy of midlife. You too can *Dream Dare Dance!*

Jan Fraser, Sally Huss, Lila Larson,
Joanne Proctor, and Sue Savage

Dream Dare Dance

Dream, dare, and dance with me,
Open your heart so you can see
All the love and joy inside of you
When you dream, dare, and dance with me.

Live your dreams from childhood
Dare to be who you are
By loving yourself
And creating those goals
It's sure to make you a star.

Dream, dare, and dance with me,
Open your heart so you can see
All the love, joy inside of you
When you dream, dare, and dance.

ORIGINAL LYRICS AND MUSIC BY JOANNE PROCTOR

Part One

Dream

The biggest adventure
you can ever take is to
live the life of your dreams.

OPRAH WINFREY

Chapter 1

Dreams

You never know
where dreams will
lead you.
The important thing
is to have them.

© Sally Huss

The Second Half

Sue Savage

*M*idlife had a way of stopping me in my idealistic tracks and saying: Look. You've been a lot of places and done a lot of things. You've acquired a lot of stuff and loved a lot of people. But who are you now and what do you want the second half of your life to look like?

At the moment, I am a middle-aged woman content with exploring what is true and valuable to me. My discoveries gather in my heart for safe keeping, always expanding and reaching out toward others.

As for what I want the second half of my life to look like? I want it to look like me. I want it to feel like me. I want it to be me. I want to live at my own pace, speak my own truth in love from an empowered heart, and pay close attention to my inner voice.

I believe if I listen to it and follow it, it will take me to where I can make the biggest difference, laugh my loudest laughs, love without fear, and find my way to becoming a peaceful, fulfilled woman.

Who are you now and what do you want the second half of your life to look like?

Starting Out

Jan Fraser

I'm a dreamer.

As a young girl, I believed I could do anything. I believed I could make doll clothes for every girl's doll in the world. I believed I could make a fortune at my lemonade stand. I believed I could win first prize for my tomatoes at the Ohio State Fair. I believed I could make other people happy by simply being with me. Such were my first childhood dreams. Some dreams came true and some didn't. That hasn't stopped me from dreaming.

How about you?

What were your dreams when you were growing up? Were they to be an "A" student, play the piano, have a successful career, experience freedom, be treated well, help other people, fall rapturously in love, swim the English Channel, grow up to be a happy woman? What were they for you?

What is your dream now?

Perhaps your children have left the nest. Perhaps you are on your own for the first (or tenth) time. Perhaps you'd like to be. Perhaps you're longing for a new career, a deeper sense of purpose, a more intimate relationship, an adventure, a new start—the possibilities are endless.

Where are you now?

Growing older often heightens our awareness that our time on this earth is, indeed, finite. Questions arise: What is most important to me now? How will I make the most of the rest of my life? What will make me happy now? What matters most?

I believe this time in life can offer an amazing opportunity—the opportunity to find and act on what matters to us most.

For some women, the act of dreaming itself now eludes them. Perhaps you too have forgotten how to dream. Perhaps you have forgotten your dreams. You are not alone.

Reconnecting to your childhood dreams can be a powerful tool in igniting the fire of dreaming now. This process can put you in touch with the world of possibility you imagined as a child, when all paths were open and the future seemed endless and filled with possibility.

Let yourself remember the hopes and dreams you had as a child. Write them down. Use detail. Visualize yourself, those around you, and what you saw ahead. What did you want for your life? What did you have in mind? What people, activities, and ideas—big and small—excited you, made your heart sing? Writing these dreams down can set your creativity in motion to find ways to actualize your dreams.

You are never too old to dream. Allow yourself to dream now.

Let the women who share their stories here inspire your own dreams.

Slow Walking

Jin's Story

I must be a slow walker. It took me five decades to realize the purpose of my life.

One snowy winter night in Korea, when I was a 12-year-old girl, I stood outside my mother's tavern with my baby brother on my back, trying to get him to sleep.

Behind the steaming glass doors, I saw my mother arguing with the town drunkards. Minutes later, when the drunkards tumbled outside, my father came out to go to work at the railroad station. With a broad smile, he patted my head.

I watched as my father set off on his rusty, old bike and slid precariously over the frozen snow. His small figure disappeared into a dark alley. Only his bicycle tracks were left behind, a thin trace in the snow.

I heard a sobbing voice swirling in my heart saying, Someday I will become somebody and take good care of you, Father.

My childhood dream was to become someone respectable who no one would dare look down on and treat badly. When I asked my sixth-grade teacher what would be considered such success, he replied with one word: "Ph.D." Thus began my dream of earning my Ph.D.

Years passed as I worked day in and day out as a housemaid, a waitress, and a factory girl in a wig-making factory. With each passing year, my hope faded until I felt such despair I was ready to let my life go. Then one day, I saw a newspaper ad for a housemaid in America.

On a gloriously sunny day in 1977, the Statue of Liberty welcomed me, heralding my new beginning. Even though I spoke little English and had only $100 to my name, I was happy. I was 22 and I had a dream.

The next six years brought me great joy and great heartache. I completed two years of college and gave birth to my beautiful daughter, Jasmine. Yet, at the same time, my husband was violent. I finally escaped his abuse the only way I could think of—I enlisted in the U.S. Army.

The U.S. Army not only provided me with a safe haven and military training, the U.S. Army paid for my formal education. While serving in the Army, I attended school part-time and raised my daughter as a single mother. Jasmine grew up as a beloved "army brat," traveling with me wherever I was stationed. We moved so many times that I had attended six different colleges and 15 years had gone by the time I received my bachelor's degree! Graduation day was a happy day indeed, but my dream was not yet in my hand. A Ph.D. still beckoned.

Just after my 40th birthday and while serving as a U.S. Army captain, I joined the scholars at Harvard to study for my master's degree in East Asian regional studies. Before I was 40, I had never even dreamed of attending Harvard. Competing with the young and the restless was a struggle no doubt, but three years later, I was still all in one piece when I returned to the Army, my master's complete.

I returned to Harvard five years later to study for my doctoral degree in international relations and history, after bidding a grateful farewell to the Army and the bright prospects of an Army major. A Ph.D., my life-long dream, was on the horizon.

While I was a doctoral candidate, I was given the chance to teach undergraduates in East Asian studies. I'm sure you'll agree with my assessment that youth know all and are never wrong nor shy about speaking their minds. Indeed, this tough, ex-soldier was scared by this challenge until it occurred to me that there was something I could talk about without fear—life itself!

Into the curious minds of my book-smart students I poured the life stories of real people living in lands far away from Harvard's ivied walls. Hoping to awaken the sense of endless possibilities within my students, I shared my own story. "We cannot choose our birth," I told them. "We cannot have more than one life. We have a choice of how to live today. Make your life the best you can. It is a chance that will never come again."

Over time, I watched many of my students reassess the meaning of life and search for their own purpose and visions. One of my student's own journey had a profound impact on my life. After completing my course, this young man took a year off from academics to work as a bartender in Shanghai. When he returned to Harvard the next year, he confessed to me that it had not been easy to make a living on his own in a foreign country. At the same time, he proudly declared that he had learned the most important lesson of his life—appreciating life's wonderful gifts promises an exciting future.

It was then that I realized the true purpose of my life—sharing hope with those who are without hope and sharing courage with those building their destiny.

To my despair, my father passed away in 1989 at the age of 69. I find solace in knowing that I was able to care for him and provide him with a better life, just as I had dared to hope so many years ago. Over the course of many years, I brought my parents, my siblings, and my siblings' families to America. They lived out their lives in a much better way than if they had stayed in Korea, and this gave me tremendous joy. My success in the U.S. Army and my acceptance into Harvard brought my father great pride. I live with the belief that he is happy, even now, knowing his daughter is living her dream and helping others, especially those in need of hope.

On a sunlit day in June, at the age of 57, I received my doctoral degree in international relations and history from Harvard. At last, I had become the person of my childhood dreams—Jin Kyu Robertson, Ph.D. My daughter, Jasmine, a Harvard graduate and a captain in the U.S. Army, stood by my side.

For those who want to live, the sky is the limit.

Give life to your dreams. It will give you a wonderful life.

What Now?

Kate's Story

*B*ecoming 50 was exciting to me. Unlike many of my gal pals, arriving at my half century mark did not make me feel old. In fact, oddly, I actually felt "new." Sharing bagels that birthday morning with my two dogs and three cats (each of whom seemed to have found heaven with every nibble) delighted me beyond words. I grinned as we munched.

That day, I became determined to spend my remaining years with the people and on the ideas most dear and important to me. Becoming 50, I thought, was just the starting line for a run that I was all too ready to enjoy and definitely win.

Well, surprise, surprise. As the saying goes, "The best laid plans of mice and men often fail." Shortly after my birthday, I moved from my home in Los Angeles, where I had lived happily for over 20 years, to Palm Springs.

Why? I thought I was in love. Need I say more? In fact, most of my 50s were spent trying to understand and survive that "love," until I finally became smart enough to dissolve it before it dissolved me. Hitting 50, though thrilling on many levels, did not mean I had become instantly wise. Ten years later, I was no closer to a life that meant something to me than I had been on that exciting birthday so long ago.

Now what? Starting over at 60. Simply put: how?

It was a question that began to burn in me. The search was on. Like a hound with nose to trail, I started out. As on that day 10 years before, I still wanted and needed to make a difference.

I wanted what time was left to count.

Meanwhile, I continued to do my heart's work. I rescued dogs and cats from shelters, took them to the vet, had them groomed, and placed them in good homes. Most of my rescues went to seniors who were lonely and grateful to have a new friend to share their lives. I delighted in these magical "re-homings."

Suddenly one morning, as I was spooning the last morsel of braised chicken from the can for one of my cat "kids," it came to me—animals!

Boing! I swear, a cartoon light bulb must have appeared over my head. No doubt about it, this was my "Aha!" moment. My love for the creature kingdom had been the one constant throughout my life. It had propelled me beyond myself into a world of service to others without my even realizing it. This was what I wanted to do with the rest my life. I promised myself that whatever I did with my later years, I would never give up helping animals and the people who love them.

In 2002, I founded the Critter Coalition, a non-profit pet assistance organization for seniors. We primarily help seniors with their vet bills, pet food, and general pet care. I'm the hands-on director of our sanctuary, Fat Quail Farm, in Joshua Tree, California. At this writing, we house and care for over 35 animals: dogs, cats, farm critters, tortoises—the list goes on and will no doubt grow.

From scooping poop to fundraising, I do it all. I love every single exhilarating (though sometimes exhausting) minute. If anyone had told me that I would be hauling hay and 50 lb. bags of dog food at age 66, I would not have believed it. But I am so glad it turned out this way.

I've come home to myself. And, yes, when the fur balls are all asleep, I dance!

What Would You Do For Free?

Katherine's Story

I am a recovering attorney.

My dream to become involved in politics and help make the world a better place led me to law school. I lost sight of that dream and my authentic self as I climbed the ladder to the top.

Ultimately, I became the CEO and president of a private trust company, only to discover that the ladder had been leaning against the wrong wall. In 2001, I left the corporate world and became an executive coach with a specialty in career management and career transitions.

The question I asked myself to discover my life's purpose was "What would you do for free?"

I received this answer: Inspire and support others to be the best they can be while discovering and leveraging their talents. I am now using my talents to live my dream as a speaker, author, and coach. As a workshop facilitator, I lead "Get Out of Your Own Way"™ beach retreats which help women break through self-imposed barriers to success and happiness.

I believe that I do make the world a better place—one person at a time.

Parlez-vous Francais?

Sam's Story

I dedicated 38 years to teaching English, social studies, business art, and yearbook in the public schools of Barstow, California. All that time, I had a dream.

I dreamed of going to France after I retired to immerse myself in French culture and language. Ever since I had been a tutor and au pair for a family in London when I was 29, I had wanted to speak French. Two years of French instruction in high school had left me with almost no conversational skills. Yet, the French language fascinated me, and I knew I wanted to learn more. Quite simply, I wanted to converse in French!

I tested the waters by going to Paris and studying at the Sorbonne for a month in the summer of 2003. Inspired by my gumption, my friends joined me in Paris for a month.

Two years later, when I was in my 60s, I returned to Paris and spent five months in a studio apartment immersing myself in the language, the food, and the people. I bought my food at a local market and rolled it home in a cart. I studied and spoke French daily, experiencing the language as a native. I met visitors from around the globe, and I conversed in French with the French. I was in heaven. I was living my dream.

Everyone who has read my "fear nothing" emails from my stay in Paris have told me how amazed they are that I could do what I did. They assure me that my "go for it" attitude and actions have been an inspiration to them.

My life now is full of ideas and actions in pursuit of dreams that had once nearly abandoned. I know better now.

I danced in my studio apartment in Paris. I danced on the Champs-Élysées. And, I dance now, back home in Barstow.

A New Life at 50

Dani's Story

When I used to hear people say that yoga is good for you, I'd wonder how anyone could sit still that long. I was a fitness instructor and my preferred form of exercise was aerobics. I couldn't imagine changing from my current way of being and thinking.

Then, while I was attending a conference just after I turned 50, I hesitantly took a class called Nia, an exercise program that blends dance, yoga, tai chi, and aikido. I experienced the wonder of yoga and loved it. What started as one class in a bare conference room has become my passion.

To this day, I am living a life filled with yoga. I am 70 years old. I teach a number of classes each week, and I receive so much from my students. My focus is "yoga for health," and I've been taking classes on polarity therapy. I love every minute of it.

By living a life of balance, embracing what life has to offer, exploring new possibilities, and dancing with joy in my heart, I know that I will never be too old to dream, dare, and dance. I believe that life is what you make it.

My life began again at 50—yours can too!

Lovin' the Body You're In

Jan Fraser

It was August 1998. I remember it like it was yesterday. It was the moment I started to love the body I'm in.

I was attending a seven-day seminar led by Jack Canfield, the co-founder of the Chicken Soup for the Soul® best-selling series. Being at the beach and listening to an inspirational speaker seemed like a perfect vacation to me—until the "Mirror Exercise."

I was in my 50s then, and my body was showing signs of having been on the planet for five decades. However, I had refused to accept that parts of me were drooping, stooping, and sagging in ways I had never even imagined possible. I was living with the changes and not seeing them. It seemed to me that over-night—and completely without my knowledge—my body was aging, never to return to the slim, tight, youthful shape of yesteryear.

I dreamed to be happy with the body I'm in.

Before Jack assigned the "Mirror Exercise" for our evening homework assignment, the training had been pretty smooth sailing. We explored our past joys, current feelings, and future goals, and I had time to reflect on me, my life, and where I was going—while enjoying the beach. But that night changed everything.

These were our instructions: Stand in front of the mirror in your dormitory room and speak directly to your own face in the mirror for five minutes with a message of gratitude for being there for yourself.

How was it possible to stand in front of the mirror and talk to myself, let alone keep a conversation going—with myself—for that length of time? What would I say? How could I not laugh and quit midway through? And how would I politely ask my roommate to leave the room so I could have the mirror to talk to myself?

Nevertheless, later that night, I found the time to be alone in our room. When I finally forced myself to stare into the mirror, I struggled for words. I'd talked to countless people in my lifetime without any hesitation, but when asked to strike up a conversation with myself, I was at a loss.

I decided to start with my eyes. Hazel, I noticed, with flecks of gold. Then, I thanked my eyes. I thanked my eyes for seeing the good in others. I thanked my eyes for looking into the eyes of other people and not at the ground when someone was trying to connect with me. I thanked my eyes for all the miracles I had seen over the years. I thanked my eyes for gazing into my lover's eyes and for seeing my babies born. I thanked my eyes for the gift they are to me.

I thanked my lips for speaking with kindness to people that day. I stared at my chin and was tempted to talk about how many chins there were. Instead, I thanked my chin for holding the lower part of my face together. I thanked my brain for processing the information that was being shared with us that week.

And on it went for five long minutes. I admit that I checked my watch several times and often scrambled for something to say to my face. I had never looked at myself in the mirror for longer than it took to put on my makeup, let alone talk to myself while doing so. But, when I finally passed the five-minute mark, I felt a tremendous sense of relief and accomplishment. I was proud of myself for completing the "Mirror Exercise."

The next day, Jack upped the ante. Our next assignment? The "Nude Mirror Exercise."

Yes, that's right. The instructions: Take off all your clothes (alone, in the privacy of your room), stand in front of the mirror, and talk to your body. The goal: to appreciate all that your body has given to you in your life. Let's just say I was not looking forward to this installment of building my self-esteem. At all.

Nevertheless, that same night I dared to do the "Nude Mirror Exercise." After dinner, I found my dormitory room vacant, and I removed my clothes.

The minute I turned to the mirror, the tears started to flow. I wept for the body that was not what it used to be and the youth that had slipped through my fingers. I cried because in 50 years I had never stood in front of the mirror and celebrated my body.

I looked at my arms. I thanked my arms for holding my mother as she died of Alzheimer's disease. I thanked my arms for holding my daughters and grandchildren long into the night when they were fussy or crying. I thanked my back for working long hours for me and my family. I thanked my belly for carrying my babies to term and delivering them to me.

I thanked my heart for keeping me standing and renewing my vibrancy every second of the day. I thanked my breasts for nursing my babies. I thanked my legs for carrying me to school, to work, to a friend's home, and through all the charity walks I had been on.

I thanked my stomach for digesting the food I sent it to receive. I was tempted to rail about my midsection, but I resisted my urge to complain.

And on I went for five minutes. Through the tears, I made a discovery—I am grateful to be in this body. I have hid it in large tent dresses, refused to look at it, and wished it would go away, but this body has not abandoned me. This body has stayed with me through thick and thin through all my years.

I truly love this body. It is mine.

I returned to training the next day a changed woman. My step was lighter. I was happier with myself. Somehow, I now treasured every bulge and wrinkle. I decided body "accents" are the new contours on the landscape of my life. They tell a story of a woman who has walked her path, however long, with goodness in her heart for others and now has messages of love in her heart for herself.

Celebrate your body. Embrace it. Love the body you're in.

Change is inevitable, except
from vending machines.

ROBERT C. GALLAGHER

Dare to Dream

Let nothing hold you back from
Exploring your wildest fantasies,
Wishes, and aspirations.
Don't be afraid to dream big
And to follow your dreams
Wherever they may lead you.
Open your eyes to their beauty;
Open your mind to their magic;
Open your heart to their possibilities.

Dare to dream.
Whether they are in color
Or in black and white,
Whether they are big or small,
Easily attainable or almost impossible,
Look to your dreams,
And make them become reality.
Wishes and hopes are nothing
Until you take the first step
Towards making them something!

Dare to dream
Because only by dreaming
Will you ever discover
Who you are, what you want,
And what you can do.
Don't be afraid to take risks,

To become involved,
To make a commitment.
Do whatever it takes to make
Your dreams come true.
Always believe in miracles,
And always believe in you!

JULIE ANNE FORD

Chapter 2

Empty Nests

The human heart
longs to be useful.
When one door closes
another door opens.

Filling the Void

Jan Fraser

There are all kinds of "empty nesters."

Traditionally, an empty nest means that all the children have left the roost and gone off to college, jobs, and life, leaving Mom with a void to fill.

It can also mean that we have arrived at our 40s, 50s, 60s and beyond with the feeling that we need to do something more with our lives. Sometimes, we hunger to create professional success in a different arena or for the first time, or to give back to the world in a way that has been limited by the time constraints of being needed by everyone else. Sometimes the loss of a job, a particular home, a beloved pet, or a family member can leave us feeling a void. A change in health or the loss of youth can also leave us feeling empty.

It is important to move on and fill your nest.

My sister, Dolly, a stroke survivor, suddenly lost her caregiver after he began hemorrhaging in her living room. My sister called 911, and he was rushed to the critical care hospital where he lingered for three weeks before he passed away. Dolly was devastated. He had been her caregiver 24 hours a day, 7 days a week for many years. They were very bonded and did everything together. Without him, Dolly felt empty and at a loss. How would she even manage without his companionship and help?

My sisters and I found an assisted-living care center for Dolly, but we worried that the loss of her caregiver would send her into a deep depression. Dolly surprised us. Somewhere inside, Dolly realized that she must move on for her own health, despite her grief. She is doing well now—she is cared for in practical ways, and she is enjoying the companionship of her new friends at the care center.

Although you may feel reluctant at first, dare yourself to move one foot in front of the other. Dream of filling your nest. Take your first steps toward realizing that dream.

This can be the perfect time. Learning something new will bring vibrancy back into your life. Learn a new language, a new skill, or volunteer at your local hospital. Giving service to someone else can often help you to take your first steps out on that limb.

When I volunteered at my local Alzheimer's Association soon after my mother died of the disease, it helped me take my mind off my own grief and allowed me to start to imagine what my life might be like without her. Slowly, I began to take the steps toward creating a living legacy that would make my mother proud. It was a way to carry on the kindness she extended to others through her nursing and her life.

One day, when I had finished speaking at a women's conference, a woman approached me onstage and asked if she could ask me a question. I answered, "Of course." After listening, connecting, and counseling with my new friend about a challenging situation she was dealing with at home regarding her husband and child, we hugged. With that hug, I sent her my strength and loving support. As I was walking away, I said to myself, "Mom, I know you're proud of me today. I helped that woman. I am carrying you and your legacy in the lifework that I am doing."

By daring to get through the time of an empty nest, dreams can evolve.

Let the stories in this chapter inspire you to fill your empty nest.

The Waltz of Your Life

Joanne Proctor

When my first daughter took her first steps just after her first birthday, I remember telling my mother how amazing it was to watch my daughter walk across the room on her own. My mother said to me, "Yes, how marvelous! But, you know, this is just the start. One day, she will walk away from you into the world."

She did, of course. Eighteen years later, my daughter had become a lovely, independent young woman, and she moved out of the house to begin a life of her own. A few years later, my second daughter, an equally lovely and independent young woman, did the same.

What a strange feeling to live with your children from birth to adulthood and then, suddenly, they're gone, away from your lap. I felt enormous loss. I missed waking up with them, sharing meals, helping with homework, going to their activities, hearing about their latest exploits, getting to know their boyfriends and girlfriends, refereeing their arguments—I missed everything about them. The house felt silent and I felt empty.

After about six months, I finally decided that enough was enough. I had to get back into action. I had to begin making changes.

First Steps

To start, I changed my younger daughter's bedroom into an office for myself. Beforehand, every time I walked past her room, it seemed like time stood still. I think I was waiting for her to return. Redoing the room and making a space for my own work helped me let go.

My next step was to try to stop hanging on emotionally to my children. It became clear to me that I was still "Mom," but my role was different now. I had to let my daughters lead their own lives. I had to let them walk away from me in more ways than geographically. One thing I did was to give them space. They could call me as much as they wanted, but I did not need to be calling them more than that. I had to let them go.

Often during that time, I thought of the saying, "When one door closes, another door opens." The other door did not open automatically for me. Time passed, and then one day, a startling thought occurred to me: I'm free! I am free to create my own life—for me. The door not only opened, the wind blew in and cleaned out the cobwebs. I realized that it was vitally important for me to build my own self-esteem and my own life independent of motherhood. The kids had started a new chapter in their lives, and now it was time for me to start a chapter of my own. This was an exciting possibility.

I was free to pursue my own dreams.

The Dream

I was then faced with some big questions: What did I really want to do? Now that I was free, what were my dreams? Did I have a midlife dream? No, I had three midlife dreams:

* Dream 1: Education

I dreamed of furthering my education to enhance my career. At that time, I was working in middle management at a non-profit organization. I was already training staff at my job, but I wanted to have the credentials to back up my skills. I realized that I wanted to become a teacher and trainer.

* Dream 2: Reiki

I dreamed of becoming a Reiki healer. I had a driving need to know more about alternative healing—healing that does not come in a pill bottle and has a spiritual element. I wanted to learn more about Reiki. Reiki is a combination of two Japanese words—"rei" which means God's wisdom or the higher power, and "ki" which means life-force energy. Reiki is a simple, natural, and safe method of spiritual healing and self-improvement using life-force energy. It is my passion.

* Dream 3: A Vacation

I dreamed of a sunny vacation. It was a fact that I had never gone away to a warm climate for a vacation. I dreamed of going someplace that was sunny, warm, and most of all, had a beach. I was not sure exactly where I was going, but I really wanted to get there.

So, those were my three dreams in a nutshell—furthering my education to enhance my career, becoming a Reiki healer, and going on a sunny vacation.

The Dare

Now for the hard part: How would I get there? How would I go back to school when I was not only committed to my job, but I needed the income? How would I find a suitable Reiki teacher? And with my tight finances, how would I ever afford a vacation while paying for my education?

I had to dare to make my dreams come true.

* Dare 1: Education

I dared to find and apply for a degree program. It was a challenge to even consider that there would be a way I could accomplish this dream. I had to dare myself to take the first and hardest step. This is what I did: I stopped just thinking about it, and I took action. I felt the fear and went for it anyway. I turned on my computer and began surfing the internet for schools that had the program I was looking for.

I discovered that there are many academic and training programs designed for people—especially women—who have other commitments. Many women enrolled in these programs have been able to continue their careers or raise their children—while pursuing their education. If they could do it, I could do it. I found a suitable program nearby with a flexible schedule. With the classes only on Friday nights, Saturdays, and Sundays, I could continue to work full-time during the week. I applied.

* Dare 2: Reiki

I dared to find a wonderful Reiki master. To become a Reiki healer, I needed to find a Reiki master or teacher skilled in the "laying on of hands." The ability to spiritually guide a person's life-force energy through the laying on of hands is passed on during an "attunement" given by a Reiki master. It is important who your Reiki master is. I searched and searched until I found Francesca, a beautiful woman inside and out who had studied Reiki with a grand master and was the granddaughter of one of the original descendents of the Usui system of Reiki. Francesca became my Reiki master.

* Dare 3: A Sunny Vacation

I dared to tell everyone I knew about my dream for a sunny vacation. At that time in my life, I was not the type of person to openly share my desires with a lot of people. However, I bit the bullet and put it out there to see what was returned. I told everyone I knew to please keep me in mind if they heard of any wonderful—and cheap—vacation packages in a warm, sunny, and sandy spot.

The Dance

* Dance 1: I graduated.

I felt a sense of power the night I graduated, as if there was no stopping me. As I stood on the stage in my cap and gown and received my diploma, all the struggling to juggle life, work, and school for the past three years was forgotten and replaced by a great sense of accomplishment. I now had the credentials to back up my experience and pursue a career in teaching and training just as I had dreamed.

* Dance 2: I became a Reiki master.

Like my graduation, becoming a Reiki master is an important accomplishment for me, but it is a more humble one. I feel blessed and grateful that I have been given this gift I can share with others. I do not have the words to express the feeling of serenity and oneness that I experience now because of Reiki.

* Dance 3: I went on a sunny vacation.

Christmas in Hawaii! Yes, at last I went away on a warm, sunny, and sandy vacation. I attracted a first-class affordable vacation to me. A friend heard about a vacation package special as it was advertised on the radio—a trip to Hawaii. I snapped it up and was on my way. As I wiggled my toes in the sand and basked in the warm Hawaiian sun, I was living my dream.

Failure is Not an Option

As I look back now, I can see how far I have come since my daughters left home—in my career, my spiritual path, and my ability to attract what I desire into my life. I moved toward my dreams with passion, focus, and a "failure is not an option" attitude. Sure there were times when I wanted stop the train and get off. But I refused to quit. Quitting was not an option.

Sometimes, that little sabotaging voice inside tried to interfere: Come on, you can't expect to carry such a load of work. You're older. It's time to take it easy. Who needs all this education anyway? Give yourself a break. I knew this voice could stop my journey toward my dreams. So, I intervened before those self-destructive thoughts could get me side-tracked.

Every time my sabotaging voice came into my head, I visualized a gigantic red stop sign. No kidding. Then, this is what I thought: Cancel, cancel. Your feed-back is not needed at this time, thank you. Then, I quickly visualized myself in three situations: receiving my teaching diploma, being a Reiki master, and breathing in the warm ocean air as I felt the sand between my toes. The more I did it, the easier and more natural it became, and the less the voices came to stop me.

That is how I did it. Your strategies for staying on track may be different and whatever works for you is great. There is no one who knows you better than yourself, and intuitively you will know best how to reach your dreams.

So, get ready. Choose a dream or two or three. Dare to follow your dreams, keep your focus, take a few dance steps along the way, and celebrate at the grand finale.

Fill your empty nest with your dreams. Wear your best dress and enjoy the waltz of your life!

Not only is another world possible,
she is on her way.

On a quiet day,
I can hear her breathing.

ADRUNDHATI ROY

Hope for Kids

Elaine's Story

When my children grew up and went out on their own, I felt a need to find a purpose greater than myself. I wanted to make a difference in the lives of children.

My dream came true when I became a volunteer for an organization called HOPE for Kids. HOPE stands for Helping Other People Everywhere, and it does exactly that. HOPE has opened orphanages in many countries, including Russia, established AIDS clinics for orphaned children in South Africa, offers affordable health care through clinics in underdeveloped countries, and reaches out to the poor within the United States.

As a volunteer, I am involved in HOPE efforts that dare me to venture beyond the comfort of my home into areas where those in need live. Over the past few years, I have passed out flyers about state health insurance programs in core areas, taught classes to underprivileged kids in Chicago, helped single mothers and their kids get to places they needed to go, served meals in shelters, and raised thousands of dollars door-to-door.

Every time I make a difference in another person's life, my heart dances.

Mount Kilimanjaro

Nina's Story

*A*t 48, I decided I wanted to create my own business, so I enrolled in Columbia University's Graduate School of Business and received my M.B.A. in finance. One of my major messages to women is that they must learn finance in order to get to the top.

After graduate school, I started Regent Capital with two investment bankers. However, over time, I realized that I much prefer running a business to functioning as a minority investor. As I began hearing women complain about the limited choice available in women's clothes, I became inspired to start my own line of women's clothing even though I had been planning to retire.

I financed the business with my own money, investing a significant part of my net worth even though I was 58. It was risky, but I wanted to get the business up and running. We launched the business in 2003, and the first year we brought in one million dollars in revenue. We plan to triple that this year. The approach I took was to first develop a strong, high-quality product and expand the business afterward.

At 58, along with starting my own company, I became a newlywed. My husband lives in Washington and I live in New York. We both love what we do and wouldn't dream of giving up our careers. We manage by making the time we have together very special.

If you think you want to start a business, you must first do something you never dreamed you could do, like climb Mount Kilimanjaro. I can assure you that building a successful business will be more difficult and take longer than getting to the top of the highest peak in Africa. I know this because I climbed Mount Kilimanjaro in 1997.

Breathe deeply and keep putting one foot in front of the other. You will be dancing in no time at all.

The Land Down Under

Maggie's Story

I always wanted to be an exceptional teacher, to create an environment in which students would be excited about learning, self-discovery, and life. My mission was to create a safe place where students could take risks and achieve success. When I first starting teaching English at a government high school in Australia, my native country, I read the faces of the kids who felt worthless, ugly, and unloved—and saw myself.

My parents were alcoholics. With little love and nurturing as a child, I believed that I was damaged and impossible to love. I felt worthless, a waste of space. Everyone else seemed more than me: prettier, smarter, better. I saw the same feeling in many of my students who were growing up without love.

I became committed to helping these children find something special inside of them. In doing so, I found something special in myself. As I watched my students begin to believe in themselves, develop a sense of worth, and achieve results they had never even dreamed possible, I felt worthwhile for the first time in my life. I mattered. I could make a difference.

With the birth of my four wonderful sons, I decided to stay at home for those early years so that I could be the main influence in their early growth and development. More than anything, I wanted to give them the love and nurturing I had not known. It was a precious time in my life.

Once my sons were on their way, rather than return to full-time teaching, I decided to train to be a transpersonal counselor and coach. I wanted to focus on helping others discover their unique gifts and talents so they could make the world a better place.

In 1998, I won a local Rotary award that allowed me to attend Jack Canfield's intense week-long Facilitator's Skills Seminar in Santa Barbara, California. In this amazing week, I learned hundreds of new skills for motivating people and was inspired by other participants who were eager to empower others to reach their full potential.

Later that year, I opened my own business in Albany, West Australia—Esteem Plus: Counseling Training and Education Centre. I lost $35,000 in my first year of business. Mainly, I was frightened to charge enough for my services. I have learned that this is not unusual for children of alcoholics who struggle with self-worth. I almost gave up and walked back to teaching, but I did not. I dared to pursue my dream.

Eventually, my business grew tremendously, and I decided to take some time off and write a book. My first book, *Saving Our Children from Our Chaotic World*, was published in 2003. I have written two others. I have been able to reach out to countless people in the Canary Islands, Scotland, England, Ireland, America, and Australia through my books.

My work has been a blessing. Helping others reach their full potential, especially those who struggle to find their innate gifts and talents, is a true joy. I have discovered that every child, teenager, and adult secretly wants to be loved and accepted exactly as they are. I have learned that we all want to make a positive difference in the world in our own way.

For that little unhappy lost child from the very bottom of "the land down under," it has been an amazing journey. We all hold that potential to help someone else find that unique part they have brought into the world. Anyone can do it every day of their lives. When we give this gift of hope to others, we also give ourselves the gift that we too are getting closer to being the best person that we can be.

I dance with the awareness that by holding true to my dream, my life is filled with joy!

Opening My Heart
Linda's Story

My life changed abruptly when my daughter moved away from home to attend college. Days were no longer filled up by my daughter's needs, musicals, costuming, science club, and carpools. I busied myself with teaching and other activities, but I wondered what else life had to offer. A relationship seemed out of the question—no time, too complicated, too old, unlikely. Looking back now, I can see that I was afraid to take a chance again. I was protecting my heart.

When I turned 53, I decided it was time to let people know they had made a difference in my life. There was a friend of mine from high school who had influenced me more than he may have realized, and I wanted to let him know. A simple New Year's card changed my life and destiny.

After finding my old friend's address online, I mailed a New Year's card to him, enclosing a letter of thanks for his impact on my life. Even though I felt a bit silly, I did it. When he sent back a simple request—Let's reconnect—our new adventure began.

We rekindled our friendship, and although I was hesitant at first, my trust increased each time I saw him. Each week, we had delicious meals together and talked for hours. Life took on new meaning for me. I felt lighter and filled with joy. I no longer had to try to busy myself with ordinary tasks to fill up my time. Eventually, love blossomed. It blossomed because I opened my heart.

Sometimes, I think of it like this: He came through the back door of my heart. I am glad I opened the door.

I dreamed of something more, dared myself to write—and send—the thank you card, and now I dance as I bake a new recipe for my soul mate. He is my friend from long ago, and now he is my soul mate. Our paths intersected and together we travel, dreaming of days ahead.

Follow Your Destiny Wherever it Leads You

There comes a time
In your life
When you realize that
If you stand still,
You will remain at this
Point forever.
If you fall and stay down,
Life will pass you by.

Life's circumstances are
Not always what you
Might wish them to be.
You may at times be led
In directions that
You never imagined,
Dreamed,
Or designed.

Rather than questioning
The direction your life
Has taken,
Accept the fact that
There is a path before
You now.

Walk your path one step
At a time
With courage, faith, and
Determination.
Keep your head up, and
Cast your dreams to the
Stars.

Soon your steps
Will become firm and your
Footing will be solid.
Keep your belief
In yourself
And walk into your new journey.

You will find it magnificent,
Spectacular,
And beyond your wildest
Imaginings.

VICKI SILVERS

Chapter 3
Life Purpose

There is a purpose
for every life
and a life
for every purpose.

What Matters Now?

Jan Fraser

We all give love in different ways throughout our lives. The passing of time can change the configuration of our families, work, and friends, but often our gaze still searches for those people and things that need us most. It is not uncommon, in the middle years, to search for a purpose in life beyond what we have known before.

There is so much we can do. Needs are everywhere. Our love and the ways we can touch and impact the lives of other people have no bounds. When we were in high school, we might have been candy stripers at the hospital or assisted at the Special Olympics with our youth group. Whatever our experience has been, service is ingrained in our hearts and in our souls. It feels good to give of ourselves, and we may have more time now.

For some, it may be caring for an ailing parent or friend. Others long to give back to the world beyond their own families in a way they were not able to do before. Making a positive difference in the lives of other people, whatever form it takes, can be a wonderful and transformational part of our middle years. It can bring great joy to us and the lives we touch.

Search for a cause, a charity, or a vision that you know will make a difference for others. That vision may be in your own home as you raise or babysit grandkids or take care of an aging relative. Perhaps you're inspired to reach out to walk for breast cancer, MS, heart disease, or diabetes. Or to volunteer at your local food bank, mentor a foster child, raise money for AIDS, or collect books for those who have none. Some women look to the larger community and create a foundation by gathering friends and neighbors united to give to others.

Whatever your focus, do not hesitate. Do not hold back. Touching hearts is part of who we are. It sustains us and builds our self-esteem while giving us grace and gratitude for the blessings we enjoy.

Let the stories of the women in this chapter inspire you to find your life purpose.

*When sleeping women wake,
mountains move.*

CHINESE PROVERB

Empowering Women
Deborah's Story

Right in the middle of my life, I found myself divorced, on my own, and ready to serve my community. Community service had always been one of my interests, but it was not until I heard a man from Mexico speak at my Rotary Club about microloans and microbanking that I found my real niche and my dream. At that meeting, I learned that one in five people in the world live on less than $1.00 a day. I thought, These people have real faces, real children, and real stories.

Unwilling to take someone else's word as fact, I flew to India and Nepal to see those faces and hear those stories myself. On the streets of India, I met a woman who borrowed $4.00 from me. She had never seen $4.00 in her entire life. With that $4.00, she bought a comb, a pair of scissors, a mirror and put her husband in business as a barber. Now she has a home and her children attend school—all because of $4.00.

Thus sprung my passion for world-wide microcredit programs. In 1997, I started the Foundation for Women, a non-profit organization dedicated to nurturing, educating, and supporting women of all ages, nationalities, and spiritual beliefs. Our microcredit programs reach more than 80,000 women in India and Africa who never had a bank account or a line of credit. In San Diego, my home base, the Foundation for Women offers business capital, encouragement, and support to families living below the American poverty line as well as women with a life-threatening illness. Whether I am in the poorest villages of Southern India or in my hometown of San Diego, I am committed to helping women reach their full potential.

My heart soars every time I see another woman moving forward. What joy I find in knowing that what I am doing makes such a difference!

Caregiving

Jan Fraser

M y mother and father were married over 50 years and made a solemn promise to each other to never place each other in a "home." When my mother started to show signs of memory loss, her doctor confirmed our worst fears—my mother had Alzheimer's.

The diagnosis hit me hard. How could this be happening to my mother? She was the intellectual in the family, daily devouring the Wall Street Journal and books of all kinds. She made all the financial decisions in her marriage. A registered nurse, she had courageously blazed a trail by defying her father's wishes for her to devote her life only to marriage and children.

Most of all, she was my mother. My dearest friend. A sweet, loving caregiver whose praise and companionship I treasured. I had dreamed that she would be with me for years and years to come—when my children were married, when her great grandchildren were born, when I needed her. The thought of her not recognizing me was unimaginable.

Shortly after her diagnosis, my mother started to show pronounced symptoms of the disease. Events from decades earlier were fresh and vivid in her mind, but she couldn't remember what happened yesterday. All too soon, what had happened a few minutes earlier often eluded her. It was painful to watch. It became clear that she needed my help.

I was newly married and living in San Diego. My parents and my job were in Los Angeles. I decided I would stay at my parents' house for half the week to help care for my mother and take the train to San Diego to be with my husband for the other half of the week.

As my mother deteriorated, the woman she had been receded from us. I forced myself to get through the most difficult days—days when life seemed to be rushing by way too quickly and the sorrow and loss were overwhelming. I discovered that caregiving can be wrenching, challenging, and backbreaking. It also contains simple gifts.

Often, as I took care of my mother, I thought of the countless times she had cared for me. Such as the time I told her about my first kiss. I was in the eighth grade, and we had just moved to a new city. Since I was the "new girl," I was especially excited to be invited to a party. At the party, I met a boy named Gary, and he asked me to walk around the block with him. While we were on that walk, Gary pulled me to him and gave me my first kiss.

Later that night, my mother was waiting up for me, snuggled in her bed. I sat down on the side of her bed and regaled her with the story of my first kiss. For years to come, she waited up for me, ready to listen to my tales, no matter how late it was. This, like all she gave, was a gift given in love.

Eventually, as my mother's Alzheimer's took its tragic course, she lost much of her memory. She did not know which day it was nor how to get dressed. Zippers and buttons baffled her, and she thought nothing of putting on her pajamas over her pants or her pants over her head. Most excruciating of all, she did not know my father, her husband of 50 years. She did not remember who he was.

One night, as I was getting my mother ready for bed, she looked up at me with her big, brown eyes. I did not know if she recognized me. I asked if she would like me to tell her a story. She said, "Oh, yes."

I sat down on the side of her bed and spun a long, elaborate tale about a prince and princess who lived happily ever after. My mother's eyes were focused on me, but she never showed or spoke any reaction to the story. At the end of my tale, she said, "There was only one thing wrong with your story."

Oh no, I thought. Had I told a bad story, aimed too low, underestimated her capacity to understand, made her feel small and simple and humiliated? I asked what she meant. "It wasn't long enough," she said.

As I tucked her in for the night, my mother asked me where my mother had been that day. I told her that my mother was with her daughter. It was Mother's Day.

The number of times in my life that my mother had told me a story are too numerous to count. Each time, it was an act of love. Now, we had come full circle. I was giving the same kind of love back to her. Isn't that what caregiving really is? No matter how difficult, it is a giving back to those who have cared for you.

I came to realize that this caring relationship with my mother was a dream that I hoped would never end. Like my story, it was a fantasy.

On my mother's last night on earth, I sat by her bed in a hospital room, and although she was unable to visibly respond to my words, I believe love and understanding passed between us. I believe she knew it was me.

Walkin' the Talk

Sue B.'s Story

*E*ight-year-old Sam walked up to me and asked, "Can you read about my anger?" Sam was asking me to read one of his answers from his workbook called "Know Thyself," a part of the "Walkin' the Talk" elementary school program I developed to teach children how to express and handle their feelings in positive ways. What a gift Sam was sharing with me. I was humbled by the way Sam and the other children in his class were embracing the journey of discovering and learning to cope with their emotions.

I dream of giving children a way of recognizing, understanding, and expressing their emotions.

For many years, I have been concerned about the way the children I have observed in my school system interact with their friends, parents, teachers, and counselors. I believe that the frequent outbursts of frustration and anger stem from children being distanced from and unaware of their own feelings.

Without a method for the children to understand what is going on inside of them, they are lost, and it often slows down their progress in school.

After 10 years of developing material and conducting training for parents, teachers, and counselors, many schools are now adopting my Walkin' the Talk program. I celebrate every time I watch a child succeed in learning that we are in charge of what we feel, and we can make positive choices about what to do about our feelings. As the students in my program begin to ask crucial questions—What am I feeling? What is important it me? Why do I do what I do? What choice do I have when I feel this way?—I am happy.

My dream continues to grow as the Walkin' the Talk program expands to impact teens, parents, neighbors, and the work force.

I dance at the end of every training day!

Serving My Country

Marlene's Story

After I married the love of my life, Bill, and became a stepmother to his three wonderful children, I was ready to pursue my next dream.

I wanted to serve my country, so I joined the military. I was proud to become part of the United States Naval Reserves Medical Core as a physician and a lieutenant. One weekend a month, I left my full-time medical practice and family life to provide medical attention to approximately 80 men of the U.S. Navy. My dream had become a reality.

In 1991, I was called to serve in a time of war. I headed for Washington, D.C. to serve in Operation Desert Storm at the Emergency Coordination Center near the Pentagon, leaving behind my family, my medical practice, and a new teaching position. There were few women doctors in the military at that time, and I was honored to be one of them. I worried that I might not be good enough, but my insecurities disappeared when I was promoted to captain!

Even though there was the real concern that I might be called to join our forces overseas, I found joy in serving and protecting my country. Providing medical attention to the passionate young men and women of the military gave me great satisfaction, and it made me happy to receive their gratitude.

Fortunately, I was never sent overseas, and when my services were no longer required, I was able to return to my family and medical practice. When I reflect on my service career, I feel a sense of pride that I was able to make a difference for my country. It warms my heart.

Now, I am free to pursue my current dream—inspiring medical students to deliver exceptional care. I dance as I write books for this purpose and travel with my Bill.

Marlene passed away on January 26, 2009. This book is dedicated to Marlene and the spirit with which she pursued all her dreams.

What I Know For Sure

Barbara's Story

I know for sure that we all possess greatness inside of us—we just need the insight, awareness, and sometimes the environment to bring it forward.

To enable and empower people to see what is possible in their own life—that is my purpose as the Director of the Bachelor of Science in Human Services at Cambridge College in Massachusetts, a program I designed just after I turned 40. My goal was to create an academic program that would give adult learners from predominantly underserved populations the education, skills, and opportunities they need to work effectively in the human services profession—and at the same time—to improve the quality of their own lives.

Most of the students in the Human Services department here at Cambridge are women, and every single one of them has faced tremendous obstacles to their education. Most struggle to earn a degree while they hold down a job, raise children, and care for parents. What happens when you get sick, laid off, or one of your children has difficulties? For many of my students, the stakes are even more critical: What happens when you live in a neighborhood riddled with violence and drugs—what toll does that take? What about women who are homeless or struggling with depression or substance abuse? What happens when you have received less than an ounce of support and encouragement through all of your life? These are but a few of the challenges our students face as they endeavor to educate themselves and improve their lives.

What is profoundly inspiring to me is how most students have not only survived, but thrived in our program, despite often insurmountable odds. When my students are provided with the skills, knowledge, and opportunities to succeed—along with true support and encouragement—they begin to see what they are capable of. It is absolutely amazing to watch what can happen as my students find their voice, develop their self-worth, and find their purpose. I don't have the words to describe what it is like to witness a woman come to believe in herself and her dreams for the very first time.

I have seen first hand the amazing transformations that can take place when women are given opportunity and real support. One of my students, Angela, comes to mind. Angela is the mother of three, and her husband has been in and out of jail repeatedly. Angela has been criticized over and over by family, friends, and social service agencies for staying married to this man, but she sticks to her guns. Angela is a determined woman. Over the course of her young life, Angela was told a multitude of times that she will never amount to anything. Yet, somewhere deep inside, Angela believed she could provide more for herself and her family. She dreamed to lift herself and her family out of poverty. She dreamed of making something of herself.

Without the privilege of a strong educational beginning, when Angela first started at Cambridge, it was not easy for her. Yet, as she lived and studied in an environment that valued who she is and what she brought to her education as an individual, as formally uneducated as she might have been, Angela flourished. Her academic skills slowly increased, hand in hand with her self-worth. She came to learn that her dreams are just as important as those of any other person, and it is okay for her to pursue her own goals.

Angela readily acknowledges that she would not have been able to graduate with her bachelor's degree without the support and encouragement she received at our Human Services department. Angela is now heading for law school. My heart sings for her.

As you can see, I know for sure that each of us has dreams and value. We are all worthy. When you create an environment that truly serves to empower and help people reach their own goals, miracles happen!

This is my life purpose. I am living my dream.

Ecstasy of the Spirit

Jan Fraser

Sometimes, a bolt of lightening ignites the spark of dreaming in our lives as it did for me in 1998. Sometimes, it can lead you to experience a joy beyond your wildest imaginings.

I attended a week-long seminar in Santa Barbara, California with a huge group of people who wanted to build higher self-esteem. Jack Canfield, the co-founder of the Chicken Soup for the Soul® best-selling series, was the trainer and mentor for the week. I listened to every word and soaked up the messages. His words inspired me, big time, and I began to dream a big dream. I dreamed I would leave my comfortable corporate job and become a professional speaker and author to inspire others as Jack had inspired me.

It was more than a career goal. I wanted my life to have purpose. To empower women to achieve more love, joy, peace, and prosperity in their lives—this is my dream and my life purpose.

After the seminar, I dared to choose a new path for my life. I used the affirmations I had learned from Jack to propel me onto the path toward my dream. I have become a speaker and author, and I believe I have inspired many women through my work.

In the *Seven Spiritual Laws of Success*, Deepak Chopra explains the "Law of Dharma" or the "Purpose in Life":

> Everyone has a purpose in life . . . a unique gift or special talent
> to give to others. And when we blend this unique talent
> with service to others, we experience the ecstasy and exultation
> of our own spirit which is the ultimate goal of all goals."*

I did not understand what Deepak Chopra meant until several years later when I was the keynote speaker at an event in Louisville, Kentucky.

The event was sponsored by the Roman Catholic Church for a group of immigrant women. Each of the women in my audience had come to America to escape torture, rape, maiming, or other heinous acts in their native countries. They had come to this conference to learn tools to acclimate to their new life in America and to build self-esteem.

I felt as if I was at a conference at the United Nations as translations were delivered in six or seven languages while I spoke in English. Some of the women shared their stories of suffering and anguish. I was profoundly moved as the courage of these women who had come to America dreaming of a better life echoed through the hotel ballroom.

How could I, a middle class woman from the Midwest, stand on a stage and make a difference in the lives of these women?

As I spoke, I noticed a woman in the audience wearing a dress ablaze with a colorful African print who carried herself with grace and elegance. She sat patiently throughout the morning session. She smiled up at me unabashedly throughout my talk, despite having only one solitary upper tooth in her mouth. I was riveted to her beautiful face. Joy and light seemed to emanate from her despite the tragedies she had surely experienced in her life.

One of the interactive exercises we did that day changed my life, striking me like a lightening bolt with a desire and a dream to do more, to help more, to try to inspire more, and to live my life purpose daily. It was the "Who Are You?" exercise.

I asked the women in the audience to choose a partner and then ask their partner the question "Who are you?" in a sincere and loving way, repeating the question in their native language over and over for two minutes. When the question "Who are you?" is asked over and over in this rapid-fire manner, it provokes many kinds of responses as it peels away the onion of who you are, until it finally reveals who you are layers down, at your core.

When the time allotted for the exercise was over, I asked the women in the audience to come to the microphone and report the very last response they had given to the question, "Who are you?"

Suddenly, the room came alive. The women started to shout to, me, rising to their feet one after the other: I am a woman of courage! I am strong! I am a mother! A grandmother! A rock! Translators joined in, shouting out for women who could not speak English: Madiha is a mother! Jaleh—a boulder! Rabuwa says she is solid like earth! A fire dragon! Aeeshah is love! The voices rose in a crescendo—Swahili, French, Farsi, Spanish and more rang out, one after the other, then all at once, until the ballroom was filled with the voices of women from all corners of the globe declaring their strength and courage and love and hope, despite all they had endured.

I was overwhelmed. I did not expect this tidal wave. Tears rolled down my face.

Later, a Swahili translator came up to me and relayed a message from the woman in the colorful African print who I had noticed earlier. The translator said, "The lady from Ethiopia wanted me to tell you, she is so happy to be here with you. She doesn't understand what you are saying (no translator present for her language) and she feels more hopeful about what is to come for her. She can see ahead today."

This beautiful woman had felt my compassion for her and was inspired by my support for her and her dreams. I embraced my new Ethiopian friend for a long time. I tried to communicate that she had made a difference in my life too. It cemented my life purpose in me.

I was experiencing "the ecstasy and exultation" of my spirit that comes with service to others.

I was living my dream.

* Deepak Chopra, *The Seven Spiritual Laws of Success: A Practical Guide to the Fulfillment of Your Dreams* (New World Library/Amber-Allen Publishing, 1994).

I define joy as a sustained sense of well-being and internal peace, a connection to what matters.

OPRAH WINFREY

All the Good

I cannot do
All the good
That the world
Needs
But the world
Needs all the good
That I can do

I cannot do
All the good
That the world
Needs
But the world
Needs all the good
That I can do

LYRICS BY JANA STANFIELD

Chapter 4
Making Choices

when the heart
and the head agree
on a direction,
the choice is good.

©Sally Huss

Choices

Jan Fraser

Middle years are exciting and pivotal. They can offer a time of great change, and with great change comes the opportunity for choices. Making choices is not always easy. Remember that everyone approaches making their life choices differently, and that is okay. These simple suggestions can help you as you face important decisions.

* Look back. Remember who and what you loved, what gave you joy, and what your dreams were before now. Reflect on what choices have brought you pleasure, pride, and joy.

* Move to the present. Listen to your soul and move forward.

* Take baby steps. Put one foot in front of the other toward your future. Rome was not built in a day.

✳ Listen to your emotions. Honor them. Do not be afraid to feel them. Your emotions will guide you on your journey.

Let the voices of the women here support you on your path as you make choices.

The World is My Oyster

Carol's Story

Working as a motivational speaker in the international arena was one of my goals that I recently accomplished. One night, after speaking to a group in England, I celebrated my achievement over dinner—with myself and my journal. What came spilling out on the pages of my journal not only surprised me, it changed my life.

As I perused the menu, I started writing about how I had always wanted to have my own business but had never done anything about it. Maybe now, I wrote. I underlined it three times. I was ready for a new goal. But what type of business? This is where I had always hit a wall, folded up the paper I was writing this dream of my own business on, and threw it in the trash. This time, I walked around the wall and kept on writing.

Maybe it was the promise of eating the sockeye salmon and haricots verts I had ordered (I was celebrating, after all), or the goal I had just accomplished, or plain old serendipity. Or maybe it was that I actually drew a wall in my journal with a stick figure walking around the wall and a big arrow pointing to the other side.

I think it was around the time the waitress brought my salad (spring greens and baby beets) that I wrote, Okay, fine. What are you good at, Carol? You're good at motivational speaking, and that's great, but what else are you good at? I listed everything I know I do well: sewing, project management, travel, mentoring, gardening, kayaking, talking to people, and more. It was a decent list. But it was a long list.

Narrow the list, I wrote. Find your passion.

That was my father's line. When I was growing up, my father always told me and my sisters that we could be anything. It may sound corny, but that's what he said. He used to throw out ideas for our future all the time, but most often at dinner. "How about an oboist?" he'd ask while delivering meatloaf to your plate. "Hardly anybody plays the oboe." Biblical scholar was another popular option. Microbiologist. Archaelogist. The first woman on the Supreme Court.

It was the 1950s. The women's movement had just begun. But my father made us feel that the world was our oyster, that we could, in fact, do anything. All we needed was passion and will.

"Dream big dreams," he'd say, while spooning peas onto my plate. "Find your passion."

So, as the waitress brought my sockeye salmon, I started a new list, a list of things that I am actually passionate about. I started the list with sockeye salmon. Was I passionate about sockeye salmon? Well, yes. But was I really passionate about sockeye salmon, I mean, could I spend each and every day thinking about it? No. As you probably predicted, sockeye salmon didn't make the cut.

Finally, I narrowed my list down to two "passion" items. Out of these two, I chose the one that it seemed I could make money with—travel. Okay, but what could you do with travel? Travel, for one thing. I'd been all over the world—Japan, India, Europe, Fiji, the Pyramids, Machu Picchu—you name it (pretty much), I'd been there. I love to travel.

"Find your passion," I heard my father say, as the waitress brought me some mousse au chocolat. (As I said, I was celebrating.)

Right. But how are you going to make money traveling? I scribbled. Cruise ship employee was out. Not for me. Naval officer? No. Worldwide bicycle tour guide. Bad knee. Becoming a travel agent or working for an airline—not my cup of tea. I did not know of anything that had not already been done that I wanted to do.

"You know, you can always be an underwater biblical scholar," I heard my father say.

My father's love for throwing out ideas for our future careers eventually crystallized into that one line and became one of our favorite family jokes. But the message was clear: You can do anything. You can even make it up. You can create whatever it is you want even if it has never been done before.

Savoring my mousse, I thought about the many women who had asked me over the years how to travel successfully with kids, a husband, a house, and a busy life. I knew the answers because I did it myself for years. Could I be onto something? If many women I already know are challenged by these issues, there must be a huge number of women who face these same challenges. If I had helped a few, maybe I could help many more. But how?

I started spilling out ideas: seminars on balancing business travel with home life, an online community that brings traveling women together, a forum to share travel tips, recommendations for travel gadgets.

And there it was. My Smart Women Travelers business was born—all by myself in England, over (a very wonderful) dinner.

My father was right. Once I found my passion, it has been full-speed dancing ahead.

Knock on the Next Door
Getrude's Story

Some say I have the Midas touch and everything I touch turns to gold. I am a married woman and the mother of three children. I am an African storyteller, poet, artist, author, entrepreneur, and the founding director of three successful companies in New Zealand: a recruitment company for medical professionals, a talent agency for African Kiwis, and a property investment company. I do have an extraordinary ability to turn my dreams into reality that also has been described as the way of the wizard Merlin. It wasn't always that way.

For most of my life, I searched for a way to escape the violence and poverty of my homeland, Zimbabwe. I was determined to find a new and better life for myself and my family, and finally, when I was 34, we left for New Zealand. With little knowledge of New Zealand life and no certainty that we would be able to stay in our new country, the prospects were daunting and unpromising.

It has been eight years now. I am feeling more at home.

Since moving to New Zealand, I have become a motivational speaker. My presentations describe my life journey and have drawn hundreds and thousands. I have written of my experiences in a book, *Born on the Continent – Ubuntu!* Ubuntu is a Zulu word which means that a person is a person through other people, or "I am who I am because you are."

I am who I am because of my mother and father. When I sat on my mother's knee in Africa, she often said, "People have two choices. They can say yes, or no. If they say no, move on and knock on the next door." From a young age, I learned to follow my dreams no matter what it took. "All you need is to dream and to dream big," my father told me. "Everything you want can become a reality."

My new dream is to eradicate AIDS in African children. I have raised countless thousands for that cause. I am determined and I will not stop until my dream comes true.

I love to dance, and my smile and energy engage others to dance with me. I will always be tireless in daring to fulfill my dreams, dancing every step of the way.

Champion of the World

Sally Huss

I was 10 years old when my father and I decided I would become the "champion of the world." In tennis, that is. It was the 1950s, and back then tennis champion meant one thing—win Wimbledon. So, my father and I set out on a long trek to accomplish that dream.

My father was a fine athlete: strong, coordinated, and focused. Born to a poor family, he had no opportunities as a young man to do anything with his athletic talent. I carried these traits and his hopes for himself in our Wimbledon dream.

George Toley, the coach of the University of Southern California tennis team and an instructor at the Los Angeles Tennis Club, became my coach. A renowned technician and savvy court strategist, George had developed many Wimbledon champions, including Alex Olmedo, Rafael Osuna, and Raul Ramirez. I was an eager and willing student. Without reluctance, I tried to accomplish what was put before me: changing grips, grooving strokes, mastering shots, training feet, and learning the offensive and defensive patterns of play. Every weekend for years, my father and I drove 115 miles from Los Angeles to Bakersfield and 115 miles back home so that I could perfect my game on the courts of the Bakersfield Racquet Club with George.

By the time I was 13, I was the number one player in southern California for my age division. When I was 15, I became the number one U.S. player in my division. After winning the U.S. and Wimbledon junior titles at 18, I was junior world champion. By my next birthday, I was a semi-finalist in the women's division at Wimbledon. The next year, I would surely win. So my parents, who were not wealthy, borrowed money to fly to London to watch me "win" Wimbledon.

As any player will tell you, the hardest round to get through at Wimbledon is the first. I did not get through the first round that year. You can imagine what dinner was like that night in Soho. It was if someone had died—me. My heart was broken. My father's heart was broken. My mother tried to minimize the situation with small talk, but it did no good. I had let them down and I knew it. Devastated, I stared at my meal.

Not long after that day, I took a hard look at this life-long dream of becoming a "champion of the world." In doing so, it became clear to me that it was no longer a worthy goal for me. It was not a dream that was going to lead to my long-term happiness and fulfillment. You see, to a competitor, winning is equivalent to happiness. If I didn't win, then how could I be happy? Perhaps one day I could win Wimbledon, but I could not be champion forever. Someone would eventually come along and beat me. If being champion was the source of my happiness, then I could not be happy forever.

That is when I changed my goal.

Through the study of Zen, dance therapy, and the influence of some very wise people, I have learned to approach my life in a very different way: joyfully, freely, and happily. Playing tennis or not. Winning or losing.

Learning to live in this way has brought me great joy. I dreamed of a wonderful man and he showed up. I dreamed of a family and our son arrived. I dreamed of an art career and galleries and products soon carried my name. My personal life motto has been one of the most popular items in my gift art line for many years: Dream big. Plan well. Work hard. Smile always and good things will happen.

My heart dances continuously and my feet join in whenever possible, whether I am on the tennis court, in my art studio, or walking down the street.

Golden Handcuffs

Kim's Story

I was stuck. I had been in the same industry for years, made a great living, owned my own home, and even drove my dream car. Yet, I was doing the same thing every day, and I was bored. I often wondered how I could do something else and still make the same amount of money. As a single woman approaching 40, I needed to support myself, but I did not want to start over.

I knew there must be more to life, but I did not know what it was or how to get it. I felt trapped in golden handcuffs.

At the same time, I wanted to find someone to share my life, but I had started to doubt it was possible. Maybe you just don't get to have it all, I thought. I have a great family, good friends, good friends, a job that pays well, my health, and maybe that's enough. My dreams of getting married and making a difference in the world were disappearing.

Then, something changed. I joined a network marketing business. Eight months later, I was almost matching my full-time income even though I was only working part-time. I was surrounded by inspiring, empowering people who had vision and dreams, and I discovered my passion for coaching and training. I left corporate America and never looked back.

My sister had asked me many times before to join a network marketing business with her, but every time, I had said, "No way." She had participated in two other such businesses, and I had never seen her make a significant amount of money. I was convinced that network marketing was not for me.

However, the last time my sister brought it up, she said something different. She told me that I could make the same amount of money but work only part-time—I could support myself and follow my passions. I started to think about the things I would do if I didn't have to go into an office, work long hours, and be surrounded by negative people. I thought about the book I had always wanted to write. I thought about playing tennis. I thought about changing the lives of other people. That's when I decided to take a leap of faith.

I have discovered that my sister was right. Everything in my life has changed. With my time back, my world has opened up. I have met amazing people who believe in pursuing their dreams, and this has inspired me to pursue my own. I co-wrote my first book and started my second. I joined a tennis league and started having fun. I have helped people change their lives by showing them how network marketing can be right for them. I have worked with people who have big dreams and have watched them begin to achieve them.

I have become a new person, alive with energy, passion, and most of all, dreams. And, I have I found my true love, my husband.

I once again believe that you can have it all. I believe it starts with taking a risk and daring to dream again. That was my route to dancing with joy.

Free to Choose

Evelyne's Story

I have had many dreams. When I was a little girl in France, I wanted to become a musician, but my father said, "Non!" And in my father's household, "Non!" meant "Absolutely not!" My second choice was to become a painter. At the age of 12, I came under the tutelage of the great French impressionist Marcel Dyf. Dyf not only became an immeasurable inspiration to my art, he filled the bill for a kinder and more loving father.

At the age of 23, after considerable studying and painting, I accomplished my next dream—I came to America. I secured a student visa and enrolled in the California Institute of the Arts, doing whatever it took to support myself. In the mornings, I studied English, and at night, I gave French lessons. Unfortunately, just as I was on the verge of getting my green card, I received word that my mother was terminally ill. I raced back to France.

It was not until nine months later, after the passing of my mother, that I could find my way back to California. However, the opportunity for my green card was over. In an effort to lift my spirits, I decided to make a trip to New York to surprise my friends, Dyf and his wife, Claudine, who were in New York promoting his art. When the Dyfs opened the door of their hotel room, they were surprised, of course, but no more than I was when I discovered the Dyfs were leaving for Paris the next morning!

Like true Frenchmen, we discussed my dilemma over a glass of wine. Then, a friend of the Dyfs who had come by their hotel to bid them bon voyage announced that he would like to offer me a job. I was on my way again, this time doing medical illustrations and graphics at Cedars-Sinai Medical Center in New York.

I have always trusted life to show me the way. At each step before me, I take a view of my life and choose my next path. Once I have a goal in sight, I work toward it by taking classes, getting diplomas, and finding work in that area. I have secured degrees in drafting, design, and interior design. Now, I am one of Hollywood's top set designers.

I won't stop here. Art direction is my next challenge.

When asked why I truly wanted to come to America, I explain, "To me, the human experience is all about change, and in France that is not possible." In France, once you pick a profession, you must stick with it, no matter how you or society may change. There is a sense of freedom in America—you can do whatever you want if you are willing to work for it. You are free to choose.

My eyes dance now as I hold up my glass to salute life and how I dreamed to be in America, to love what I do, and to be happy where I am going. Bonnne chance!

Wind in Your Sails

Jan Fraser

$\mathcal{M}$ idlife is about making choices. Do not be dissuaded from your dream. When I was in my 40s, I decided to become a flight attendant. This was a dream that I had wanted for a long time, however, my family had come first and my dream had faded. As my daughters became adults, I dusted off my dream and discovered that one airline was hiring "mature" women attendants.

I dared to make this long-time dream real. Since the airline was only hiring bilingual flight attendants, I dared to learn Spanish. I was hired, graduated from a strenuous training program, and became a flight attendant at 42 years of age. I danced in the aircraft aisles.

Not everyone I knew was supportive of my decision to pursue this career. One friend told me it surprised her that I wanted to be in such a "shallow profession." I told her that I would let her know if it was shallow or not if I was able to survive the training and graduate. I did graduate and I was thrilled to be the newest "sky angel." I loved working as a flight attendant, and I am happy to this day that I did not allow other people's opinions drag me down.

Have people in your life judged what you want to do and taken the wind out of your sails? Make sure you surround your dream with supportive family and friends. Gain momentum for your dream by doing the research and talking to experts, and then make your best decision. Sometimes, you must put the wind in your sails yourself.

There are countless worthy endeavors to take on in midlife. Maybe you dream to start a business, go back to school, or adopt a child. Maybe you dream to start a charitable foundation, write a book, or survive a life-threatening illness.

What is your dream?

Whatever your dream, we stand with you. As you nurture your budding dream in your heart, we support you. You can gain support and coaching at your local Dream Club® chapter.

Here's to the joy of dreaming in midlife!

Dance for yourself.
If someone understands, good.
If not, then no matter,
go right on doing what you love.

LOIS HURST

What If You Saw Yourself as a Wise Woman?

What if you saw yourself as a wise woman?
And you accepted every decision you made
Without second guesses and regrets
Knowing it was "perfect" given the information you had
And the inner counsel you consulted?

What if you saw yourself as a wise woman
And whenever you got scared or angry or fearful
You were able to step back from that fear
And observe it
And not become it?

What if you saw yourself as a wise woman
And every time to looked in the mirror
You saw a radiant spirit-light
That touched your skin, your face, your form
With beauty and nobility?

What if you saw yourself as a wise woman
And loved yourself with a big wide love
No matter what you saw
Or what you did
Or who you encountered?

What if, for a moment, a day, a lifetime
You saw yourself as a wise woman
And acted, always, from that place of grace
UNKNOWN GIFTED POET

Chapter 5

Finding a Dream

Each dream takes
the dreamer beyond
herself and she is
better for it.

©Sally Huss

What is My Dream?

Jan Fraser

*I*met Paula as she was competing in the Transalpine-Run in September 2008. This grueling race—a two-hundred-mile run over eight days up staggeringly high mountain peaks in Germany, Austria, and Italy—is not for wimps. Many strong men had already broken bones, torn knees, and injured ankles. Few women teams were competing. Paula, and her running partner, Susan, ran on. Paula was 50 plus.

Awestruck, I asked Paula if I could include her story in Dream Dare Dance! I knew it would inspire many women to go for their dreams.

Paula's next question shocked me. She asked, "Will there be a guide in your book about how to find your dream?"

My mouth dropped open. I said, "Paula, you've already completed one Transalpine-Run, you are running in a second, you inspire women in London to run and exercise and you're asking me how you will figure out your dream? Aren't you living your dreams now?"

"Yes," she said. "But, this September I will have an empty nest as my daughter goes off to college. I need to find my next dream. I need to know how I will know what my next dream is."

Even those who have accomplished one dream, no matter its size, sometimes need help with the next. Many of us need help figuring out our first dream. Do not let this deter you from your desire to dream.

Let the stories in this chapter guide and inspire you in your search. Anything is possible!

X-treme Taekwondo

Estella's Story

*W*hen I was a young girl, a devastating earthquake nearly destroyed the area where my family lived in Nicaragua, and hundreds of children were left out on the streets to fend for themselves. My family found sanctuary in the United States, but my memories of those homeless children haunted me for years to come. I began to dream that someday, somehow, I would wrap my arms around every unloved child in the world.

After studying classical piano in college, I married and became the mother of four beautiful boys. In my limited free time, I began to take small steps toward pursuing my dream. I started out by teaching Kindermusik classes to preschoolers. As my classes grew, I discovered my love for working with children who are more difficult to reach, those with ADHD, autism, developmental delays, and other challenges. As many of these children with special needs bloomed from both experiencing music and receiving my tender care and respect, I realized that I had found the kids who I want to wrap my arms around.

Years later, my husband and I began to dream of opening a school that would cater to children of all ages with and without special needs. Who knew that the inspiration for the kind of school that might be would come from one of our favorite family activities—taekwondo? Along the way, our whole family had fallen in love with taekwondo, and my husband and I began to dream of combining this passion with our passion for special needs children. Eventually, we developed a wonderful program called X-treme Taekwondo—taekwondo to music!

After many years, my husband finally dared to quit his job, I dared to stop teaching Kindermusik, and we opened our own school. Now, I am pursuing my dream full-time, teaching X-treme Taekwondo to children of all ages and needs.

Many of my students come into class feeling defeated and beat up by other people in their lives. Many of these same children do not want to leave when class is over. I may not be wrapping my arms around the children of the world, but I have a warm, tight grip on those who pass through the door of my school.

Together we dream, dare, and dance every day

Australian Walkabout

Deb's Story

*H*ave you ever noticed how dreams are contagious, just like the impulse to chuckle when you hear another person laugh? I caught my dream from my husband.

As my husband approached his milestone birthday of 50, he made plans to leave his lifetime career to pursue something new—a passion he had yet to discover. For almost five years, he dreamed about "stepping into a void" where no preconceptions could restrict his direction. My husband's enthusiasm and openness to change allowed me to realize how much I too longed for more balance, adventure, and playfulness in my life.

After months of brainstorming and planning, we cast the die and embarked on a family-size adventure. My husband left his profession, and I closed my successful 25-year psychotherapy practice. We packed up the house, the children, and our dreams, and we moved to Australia for almost a year—a walk-about to find ourselves!

We landed in Melbourne and drove up the eastern coast to Byron Bay where our first apartment turned out to be next to a nude beach! Our son was quite discreet, keeping his eyes straight ahead yet somehow managing to see the same sights his dad. Our daughter was more vocal, running up to me one day yelling, "Mom, Mom! I just saw my first nude bather!" My glance followed my daughter's pointing finger, and there, playing in the sand, was a naked boy about her age. We were all on a big, new adventure.

Yet, as our new-found freedom began to replace the responsibility and obligation we were so used to, guilt set in. Disturbing my peace, my mind chattered, Why me? I've done nothing to deserve all this! Why all this goodness? I went in search of an answer and finally realized that our adventure had nothing to do with worthiness—every human being on the planet is worthy of having whatever it is they long for. Our Australian holiday manifested because my husband and I had created the intention and had taken action to make it happen. It was that simple. Anyone can do the same.

In 1954, Lillian Smith wrote, "No journey carries one far unless, as it extends into the world around us, it goes an equal distance into the world within." Her words rang true for my Australian journey. During the most amazing year of my life, I produced no professional, financial, or community accomplishments. In the past, I would have evaluated such a time as empty. However, the rich experience of being myself—and letting that be enough—transformed me forever. My Australian journey carried me many miles from home and many miles within myself.

Sometimes I wonder what my life would have been like without my Australian walkabout, and I can not even imagine it. When I returned from Australia, I decided to close my psychotherapy practice permanently, write a book, and enjoy life!

Just Do It

Peggy's Story

*F*ive years ago, when I was teaching yoga to seniors in Peterborough, New Hampshire, I asked one of my students a question: "What do you tell people you know about how to get started in yoga?"

"Just do it," Jo replied, her blue eyes twinkling. Jo was 97 then. She is 102 today and still going strong.

Jo is one of 30 seniors who regularly attend my yoga class called "Gentle Stretch Yoga." When the class started 20 years ago, the average age of the participants was 79. The class has been going strong ever since, and many of those first participants are still bending and stretching every week.

The inspiration for my second professional dream, "Yoga for the Rest of Us," arrived in the most unexpected way from that very yoga class. One of my loyal students suggested I make videos for the class to use when I was out of town.

I followed her suggestion, and ten years later, that small undertaking for my beloved yoga class has grown into the "Yoga for the Rest of Us" nationwide brand that it is today—a PBS and home-video yoga series for all ages and abilities.

Initially, a friend of mine introduced me to an executive producer of public television specials. She had reservations about my "Yoga for the Rest of Us" idea, but my enthusiasm prevailed. With my own money backing the project, we eventually partnered with the PBS station in Boston, WGBH, to make a twenty-minute documentary featuring five of my students, including Jo, and a three-part, instructional home video to be given away during WGBH's pledge drive to encourage membership.

When the show was aired, the audience response was off the charts. "Yoga for the Rest of Us" was an instant hit. Even today, that very program continues to raise money for public television nationwide.

The best part for me is that my class size has expanded through both PBS and home videos to include thousands of eager students. My dream of helping people become more comfortable and confident in their bodies continues on.

I stretch, dance, and "downward dog" with delight, happy that my dreams have found their way to triumph. As with yoga, it is with life. You must dare, as Jo says, to just do it.

Visiting the Queen

Diana's Story

I have had many dreams. At seventy-something years, when I look back on my life, I am struck by how many have come to fruition before my very eyes. What a wonderful life it has been!

When I was a young girl, I was infatuated with Her Royal Highness Princess Elizabeth and Her Royal Highness Princess Margaret. As a Canadian, Princess Elizabeth and Princess Margaret were my princesses, just as King George VI was my king. It was the stuff of dreams. Twenty scrapbooks scattered the floor of my room, each chock-full of newspaper clippings, Life magazine photographs, postcards, stamps—anything and everything I could find on these two real life princesses. I chronicled their every move in the pages of my scrapbooks.

As you might imagine, I longed to attend the coronation of Her Majesty Queen Elizabeth II in Westminster Abbey on June 2, 1953. It seemed like a fantasy to most people I knew, but by babysitting at twenty-five cents an hour, I finally amassed the sum of $1200 and set off for London with my mother and cousin. I was 18. Perhaps you can picture our elation as we waved madly to the young Queen when her landau carriage passed the stands in Hyde Park after her coronation.

Our adventure had only begun. Stored safely inside my light blue handbag, I had an invitation to the Queen's garden party at Buckingham Palace. My father was a lawyer in Ottawa, and he knew the Canadian ambassador, who kindly arranged our invitation. My mother had stayed up for nights and nights sewing a dress for me from a McCall's sewing pattern that would befit a royal garden party. It was made of a glorious light blue and white flowered print, and I wore a matching light blue wide-brimmed hat with a blue satin ribbon. And so it was that I walked through an arbor covered in roses into the royal garden. Moments later, I watched as Queen Elizabeth II awarded (the very dashing) Sir Edmund Hilary for his recent conquest of Mount Everest. Afterward, I was introduced to Sir Edmund Hilary, and we shared refreshments in the garden at Buckingham Palace. It was beyond my wildest girlhood dreams.

After leaving England, we went on to visit Denmark, Switzerland, France, and Italy, and my passion for travel was born. I wanted to travel the world.

Saving the money to do so—through babysitting, a job at Bell Telephone, and holiday gifts—took me three years. Yet at the age of 21, I traveled the world for nine months, just as I had dreamed. My trip started in Singapore, where I stayed with family friends, then on to Hong Kong, Japan, Cambodia, Thailand, Israel, Lebanon, Turkey, India, Germany, Italy, and England! It was one of the happiest times of my life.

Once I returned to Canada, I dreamed of becoming a teacher, but I avoided applying to university for many years. My brother was always an exceptional person, and I lived in his shadow, unable to believe that I could compete with his brilliance. However, while living at home for three years, I became more determined. I applied to a one-year teaching credential program in Winnipeg, far from my family. When the admissions committee informed me that my high school mathematics courses were insufficient for admission, I studied twelfth-grade math in summer school. Afterwards, I was accepted to Teacher's College and moved west to Winnipeg.

I earned less than $200 a month as a teacher after I received my diploma. I lived frugally and managed, struggling with the fact that I would have to attend university if I wanted to earn more money as a teacher. How could I possibly support myself during three more years of study? I was determined to find a way, and in the end, I received a $1200 scholarship, worked part-time jobs, and shared a third-floor apartment while earning my degree. The refrigerator was on the first floor of the apartment building and the shared bathroom was on the second floor. It amazed me how well I could adapt when clear on my goals.

After three years of study, I passed my last final exam. I was 31. My parents and my brother flew to Winnipeg for my graduation, and we celebrated, ate, and danced!

Now, when I look back on my life, I am struck by the dreams I pursued, the dares I took, and the dance I always felt inside of me when I achieved my dreams. I can see better now what I valued all of my life: independent thinking, lifelong learning, persistence, family, and friends. What lessons I have learned and what fun it has been.

Sometimes, as I sit here now, I feel like a queen!

The Passion Test

Jan Fraser

*P*assion for what you are doing can make life smooth and seamless. Even though there may be bumps in the road, you don't feel them nearly as much when you are living your passion.

How do you find out what your passion is? Try the "Passion Test."*

When the Passion Test was first introduced to me, I loved it from the start. It is a simple way to identify your life purpose and dream. Here is what you do:

First, make a list of the 10 things that you think will make your life complete, that is, it feels like if you accomplished these 10 things, you would feel your life had meaning and your dreams had come true. If it is difficult for you to come up with these things, try thinking of 10 things that you really enjoy doing.

Now, start with the first item on your list. Compare the first item on your list to the second item on your list and make a decision about which is most important to you. It can help to ask yourself which one you'd rather be doing. For example, which would I rather be doing right now if I had a choice—gardening or teaching?

Next, compare whichever one wins out, that is, whichever one is more important to you or the one you'd rather be doing, to the third item on your list and decide which is most important between those two. Compare whichever emerges as the most important in this match up to the next item on your list, and so on down the list, until you get to number 10.

That last surviving passion, the one that has bested all the others, is your number one passion.

You can repeat the exercise to find your number two passion and so on.

Take the top five passions that you have come up with and write a paragraph about each of these passions in your journal or notebook. Answer the following question for each of the five passions identified: What does that passion look like? Write as much detail as possible for each one.

The Passion Test is an excellent way to reveal your true passion to yourself at that moment in time. You can take the test every few months because the results change as your perspective changes.

Try the Passion Test. It may surprise you!

Janet Bray Attwood and Chris Attwood, *The Passion Test: the Effortless Path to Discovering your Destiny.* (Fairfield: 1st World Publishing, 2006.)

Recognizing Your Dream

Marcia Wieder

A dream is a hope. When you dream, you imagine something you would like to happen very much. It is a strongly desired goal or purpose.

Here are 10 ways to begin to recognize your dream and the path to what matters to you most. Use them as you explore and seek out your dream.

Passion

Passion simply means a very powerful feeling. If you are excited about a potential opportunity and perhaps can't even sleep, it's worth taking a closer look. If you feel energized and alive when you think or speak about a possibility, take the time to investigate.

Thinking

If this idea or possibility is something you find yourself thinking about a great deal, even when you are engaged in other activities, this could be your dream.

Signs

Pay attention if it feels like something or someone is pointing you in a certain direction. Some people feel they receive signs or signals that show them their way. Notice what's happening. Follow the signs.

Clarity and Confusion

You may feel completely sure or unsure about whether something is for you. Both are fine. Although most of us prefer clarity, confusion can mean you're just turning something over in your mind. Confusion and fear are often present when we are ready to make a big change in our life. This happens when you are actively looking, thinking and feeling. Explore the idea that makes you feel this way.

Ease and Grace

When something seems to happen effortlessly it can mean that it is the right thing for you at this time. There's a different kind of energy around something that's right, even though you may hit some snags. Learn to recognize this feeling. Learn to move with it. Go with the flow. See the blessing and walk towards it.

Intuition

Sometimes we know something is right in our bones. We know because we know. Confidence is the ability to trust in oneself. You can develop this place inside of you by acting on your intuition. If this feels right to you, even if you can't explain it, go for it. Even in some small way, follow your intuition. Take the first step.

Shortcuts

If a quicker, easier way presents itself to you, pay attention. This may mean it is the right time and place for you. You may not fully understand why a particular door has opened for you, but peek inside.

Connections

When it feels as if all the right people are showing up, take a leap forward and get a closer look. Everything happens for a reason. If certain people are willing and able to venture with you, why not?

Just for You

When all of your life experience makes you the perfect person for this endeavor, and it feels like this is a dream come true, seriously consider this opportunity now. Everything you have done in your life has prepared you to be uniquely you at this moment in time. If you feel you are perfect for the job, most likely, you are.

Heart Songs

When what you are considering makes your heart sing and the thought of it brings a smile to your face and feeds your soul, this is your dream.

Used with Permission from Marcia Wieder, CEO/Founder of Dream University®.

A Place to Dream

Jan Fraser

*W*hen I want to dream, I go outdoors. I breathe in the fresh air at the beach, the mountains, the lakes, the trees, or the fields. I find peace, joy, and clarity there.

This December, in Bermuda, I walked to the ocean. I felt a need to renew my dreams and dare myself to move forward on those goals. Get going was what I needed to do. I grabbed my hat, a snack, my journal, and walking shoes. I was on my way.

I sat down on a six-foot-high rock formation at Elbow Beach and felt like the queen of all I could see. Glorious sunshine warmed my face, and I felt a fine mist of sea spray. It was a heavenly spot to pull out my journal and start to write what was in my heart for my dreams. Here is a portion of my writings that day:

With a deep breath I breathe in life and all the joyous happy moments I've experienced in my life. Countless moments are now memories. Right now, I am only seeing joyful ones. They are flooding my mind now like the waves coming into shore, wetting the base of my rock throne wave after wave. The waves are like my life of living and dreaming. There is no wear date on dreaming. Waves come in one after another. Women like me all over the world are dreaming dreams now and will never stop. Their dreams, too, just keep coming in, like the waves at Elbow Beach.

Our legacies are like the ocean waves coming in—they will continue long into the beyond. It is our privilege to dream and help inspire our sisters, partners, children, family, community, and the world to dream too.

Find a place to dream. You never know what you will discover there.

Wake Up and Dream

Every life is meant for living
Every song is to be sung
Every gift is meant for giving
It's the same for everyone

For the world was built by dreamers
Dreams are real and so it seems
That this world was meant for dreaming
If we just wake up and dream

You can wait a lonely lifetime
For a knock upon your door
Ships are safe inside the harbor
But is that what ships are for
All the world was built by dreamers
Dreams are real and so it seems
That this world was meant for dreaming
If we just wake up and dream

There's a time for every person
There's a space for everything
And from every situation
What we take is what we bring

You can wait a lonely lifetime
For a knock upon your door
Ships are safe inside the harbor

But is that what ships are for
All the world was built by a dreamer
Dreams are real and so it seems
That this world was meant for dreaming
If we just wake up and dream

LYRICS BY THOM BISHOP AND ED TOSSING
PERFORMED BY JANA STANFIELD

Part Two

Dare

If I Were Brave

What would I do if I knew that I could not fail
If I believed the wind would always fill up my sail?
How far would I go, what could I achieve
Trusting the hero in me?
If I were brave I'd walk the razor's edge
Where fools and dreamers dare to tread
Never lose faith, even when losing my way
What step would I take today if I were brave?
What would I do today if I were brave?
What if we're all meant to do what we secretly dream?
What would you ask if you knew you could have anything?
Like the mighty oak sleeps in the heart of a seed
Are there miracles in you and me?
If I refuse to listen to the voice of fear
Would the voice of courage whisper in my ear?
What would I do today if I were brave?

LYRICS BY JANA STANFIELD AND JIMMY SCOTT

The key to change is to let go of fear.

ROSANNE CASH

Chapter 1

Courage

A leap of faith
may just be
an act of courage,
but still fun!

Feel the Fear and Do It Anyway

Joanne Proctor

I believe that you're never too old to make your dreams actually happen. There are times, however, when each of us questions our ability to reach our goals. Doubt starts infiltrating our thoughts: I can't do it. I'm too old. The goal is too big. This is too hard. I don't know how. I will fail. Learning how to cope with these destructive thoughts is an essential tool in succeeding in whatever you want to do.

Daring to face and conquer the challenges before you, whatever they may be, is part of the journey to your dreams.

Eight months ago, I was asked to give a keynote address that would kick off a conference to motivate professional women. It was a wonderful opportunity for me, but it was a big stretch. I had never been a keynote speaker at a major conference before and never in front of such a large audience.

I said yes even though I was afraid. 400 women is 10 times the number who had attended my prior workshop. Doubts flooded my mind: Could I pull this off? Could I inspire 400 women to be successful in their lives? Would my message be powerful enough to light their fires?

I had to dare to believe I could make this dream come true. I had to dare to *Feel the Fear and Do It Anyway®*, as the author Susan Jeffers so aptly put it.* So that's what I tried to do. I decided to create a strategy to eliminate my self-limiting thoughts and fears so that I could accomplish this goal. My strategy had four basic elements:

Affirmation
Visualization
Preparation
Cancellation

Here's how I enacted my plan:

Affirmation

I created affirmation statements and posted them in my environment:

* I am completely confident in everything I do.

* I can accomplish anything I set my mind to.

* I achieve success in whatever I try to do.

* I can easily motivate my audience to greater success.

* I can inspire my audience because I am speaking from my heart.

Visualization

I visualized myself giving my speech. I could see my audience of 400 women and feel their energy. I could see my own confidence as I gave my speech. It was my dress rehearsal.

Preparation

I was prepared. The night before the event, my PowerPoint presentation was ready. My experiential exercises were rehearsed and cued. A script that I was confident would build self-esteem and peak performance in my participants was in my hand.

Cancellation

I used a technique called "cancellation" or "canceling" for getting rid of those self-defeating, dream-crushing thoughts. The morning of my speech, as I showered, negative thoughts came on strong: What a joke! Who are you kidding? So, I said—cancel, cancel—to myself. It made me laugh and it reduced my negativity and stress. Then, I replaced the negative thoughts with the positive affirmations I had been practicing. It is a powerful technique that works.

As I finished my shower, I visualized myself standing on the stage in an enormous ballroom confidently giving a flawless speech. In my vision, 400 women rose to their feet in a standing ovation, cheering wildly. Dream on sister, you might say. I thought it'd be cool.

I arrived at the conference early and parked in a remote spot so that I could quietly focus and center myself before going inside. I closed my eyes and focused my thoughts on my breathing. As I took in a breath to the count of four, I felt the air enter my body and my abdomen expand. Then I held my breath for another second and exhaled through my mouth to the count of four. I repeated this three times.

Then I checked my lipstick in my visor mirror and made eye contact with myself. Out loud, I affirmed, "I am easily connecting with the audience while presenting my first keynote presentation."

I was ready. Now, it was time to act "as if" I was the top-notch keynote speaker—confident, captivating, and brilliant.

Once I stepped up to the podium, I took a deep breath, centering myself, and gazed out at my audience. I knew that I could make a difference in the lives of each of the women sitting before me.

And then, lo and behold, I gave my speech.

Now, you may not believe it, but this is what happened next: The audience jumped to their feet and applauded. It was a standing ovation. I was humbled. I was exhilarated.

I had felt the fear and done it anyway.

* Susan Jeffers, *Feel the Fear and Do It Anyway* (New York: Random House Publishing Group, 1987.)

Sky Diving

Jan Fraser

When my friend Jennifer, a registered nurse in her 20s, asked me to jump out of an airplane over Hoover Dam and Lake Mead with her, I was twice her age and then some. I agreed to accompany her to the jump site, but I swore that I would *not* take the leap myself. After all, I was a mature woman.

Well, after one hour of ground school, I was donning a flight suit, goggles, and a limp, leather, "Bullwinkle" helmet. The outfit was unremarkable and unattractive.

I stood on the tarmac and looked up at the plane. Was I actually going to sit inside an old rickety aircraft while a youthful (and handsome) pilot flew us to 14,000 feet? Moments later, I sat down on the floor of the plane, my back to the instrument panel. I shivered with fear. And it was not a hot flash.

It took half an hour for the old plane to climb to 14,000 feet, the highest possible point you can free fall without oxygen. Our pilot, Sean, opened the door (as I wondered why he wasn't at the controls) and announced that I would be the first to jump. "Why me," I asked. "Why do I have to go first?" Sean explained that I was closest to the door and needed to move out first. I told him I would be happy to move to another spot. "No room to change places," he said and clipped Brad, my brawny tandem-jumping expert, to my back harness.

I forced my legs to stand up and move me to the door. Brad told me to put my right foot outside the aircraft onto the wing. It looked like I would have to do the splits. I had never done the splits, not even in high school. After three earnest but failed tries, I forced my foot toward the wing. I was terrified. I looked back at Jennifer who grinned from underneath her "Bullwinkle" helmet and gave me two thumbs up. I looked down at the earth far below. I saw Hoover Dam and Lake Mead. I thought, I am a swimmer. If anything goes wrong, I will swim to shore.

In ground school, we had been taught to arch our arms and legs back, simulating a banana curve. I had never asked what happened if someone didn't arch their back. Frozen, I started saying a mantra to myself that I had learned once: Stop, Challenge, and Choose. I had used this mantra one time so far. It had helped, but then again, I didn't have my foot on the wing of an airplane 14,000 feet above the ground. "Okay," I said to myself. "Stop yourself and breathe." (I did.) "Challenge yourself to do what you have never done before." (I moved to the exit door.) "Choose to do it." (Jump!)

Then Brad jumped too since he happened to be attached to me at my shoulder harness.

Suddenly, there I was, staring wide-eyed at the great blue sky. Flying. I had no fear. Air whooshed through my body. White noise filled my ears. Calm and a sense of well-being overtook me, accompanied by a tremendous sense of accomplishment. I had jumped.

About 60 seconds later, our parachute opened, and everything became quiet and peaceful as we floated along. I felt in charge, as if I was a princess surveying my realm from a high vantage point. "This is fantastic," I chattered away. "Amazing! I love this! Can you believe it?"

We floated gently to the ground for a textbook landing with our toes pointed up. And then, you know what happened?

I danced.

Here's what I was lucky enough to learn by jumping out of a plane:
- The fear of doing the thing is 100 times worse than doing the thing.
- Watching someone jump is not as much fun as jumping yourself.
- "Stop, Challenge, and Choose" will get you through.
- Handsome pilots can make all the difference.

Let the stories in this chapter inspire you to meet the challenges before you.

I have accepted fear as a part of life.
I have gone ahead despite
the pounding in my heart
that says: turn back.

ERICA JONG

A Life of Courage and Grace

Lila Larson

On a cool September day, I sat with my mother as she made a trip through her past. At 91, she seemed serene, and her memories were as fresh as if they had happened the day before. I was struck by the courage she displayed throughout her life as she faced one enormous challenge after another, challenges that another woman may not have weathered with such hope and grace.

Come with me now as I recount the story my mother told to me.

Years and years ago, my mother was pregnant with her third child after suffering a miscarriage three months earlier. She was relieved to have just passed the first trimester of this pregnancy. Imagine her horror, then, when she fell as she got out of bed. Her six-year-old daughter was across the hall and yelled for her father to come quickly. He leapt up the stairs and helped get her back into bed.

The local doctor thought my mother was experiencing symptoms of polio and recommended she consult a specialist in the nearest large city. The specialist disagreed with the local doctor's diagnosis. He believed my mother had water on the knee and recommended surgery. She was in a quandary, but she agreed to the surgery.

After returning home, a hospital bed was set up for her in the main-floor dining room. She could not climb the stairs to the second-floor bedroom nor could she make it downstairs to use the chemical toilet in the basement. She had two children under seven, and my father's full-time job as a minister required he be available to respond to the demands of his congregation. A woman came by during the day to help care for the children.

After some time, two of my mother's friends took the bus from the city each day to help her learn to walk again. One friend held an arm around my mother's waist while the other friend kneeled on the floor and pulled my mother's feet forward, one at a time, while my mother grasped the arms of a dining room chair. She was determined to learn to walk again. She was not going to allow someone else to raise her baby.

Yet, one of my mother's legs splayed to the side even after she recovered from the surgery, and her lower abdomen had no muscular control. A third diagnosis confirmed her worst fears—she had polio. It was polio that had affected her from the waist down—surgery had not been necessary. When she finally did learn to walk again, she shuffled.

My mother was grateful to walk again.

A challenge of a much different kind followed soon afterward. A flood threatened the town where our family lived. Women, children, and the elderly were evacuated just before the bridge to town was flooded. My mother took the children to stay with her in-laws in a tiny bungalow in the city nearby.

Yet the Red River continued to rise, and the entire city was soon forced to evacuate. My mother and the children found safety in the country at her parents' home. After a month, our family was able to return home, but the house had suffered substantial flood damage up to the first-floor windows. Fortunately, townspeople had helped my father carry the main-floor furniture to safety on the second floor where our family lived for some time.

After the flood, mice were rampant in the house. My mother often woke at night to find mice playing on her coverlet. She and the mice were not friends.

My father began to repair the house while fulfilling the demands of his work and looking after the children. One day, while he was working under the floor to install insulation, my sister opened up the back door, realized that the back stairs had been washed away in the flood, and tried to close the door again. A gust of wind came up and whipped the door back against the house. She was flung twenty feet from the house, landing on a pile of vile mud from the flood.

My mother's heart ached when her husband told her what had happened. How could she not learn to walk better and be there for her kids? She doubled her efforts to walk, and by the time her third child was born a few months later, she walked with only a slight limp.

My mother gloried in the safe arrival of her third baby, a son, and was delighted to be able to move about to care for him.

My mother was grateful her family had a roof over their heads.

Later that month, my father was offered a job in the nearby city. The job would require him to travel around the province, leaving my mother with three children and no car. They could not afford a second car. After much deliberation and soul searching, the family moved to a one-and-a-half story home in the city that was within walking distance to schools, stores, and bus routes.

My father and his relatives quickly turned a room off the kitchen into a large bedroom and a pantry into a bathroom so that my mother wouldn't have to climb stairs.

The children began their fourth school in less than seven months, and soon, my father began to travel for his job. Sometimes he would be gone for a few days, other times it was a week or more. My mother found ways to manage, and even the youngest ones pitched in.

My mother felt blessed that they all had one another.

It was hard for my mother to believe it when yet another tragedy struck the city—a sweep of polio. There were two strains: one that attacked the upper respiratory system, and one that affected the lower abdomen and legs. Those with severe upper respiratory cases were placed in an iron lung which breathed for them. Families were advised to avoid public places.

Yet, my mother knew what polio felt like, and she wanted to help. So, she pulled her nursing uniform and cape from the trunk, polished her nursing shoes, got her shots, and worked in a nearby hospital with patients in iron lungs.

My mother felt fortunate to be well enough to give back the care and support she had received when she was ill.

My mother was grateful that her family survived, and that through it all, they still shared the simple joys of living.

Soon after, my mother was pregnant again, and she worried that her polio would harm her unborn baby. Would this baby be impacted by whatever might remain in her body from the polio virus, even though her third child was not? Was she strong enough to carry full term?

My mother was overjoyed when she was blessed with a healthy baby girl.

Many years have passed since my mother's fourth and last child was born. The house damaged in the flood has been condemned and torn down. The children have grown up and have their own families. My mother has turned 91.

My mother says that she has been blessed with a wonderful life—a loving husband of 66 years, four precious children, seven grandchildren, and five great-grandchildren. Her dream of having a family and living to enjoy them has been fulfilled. Despite all the hardship she has experienced in her life, she is happy.

"What better life could I have lived?" she asked on that cool day in September. "None!" she answered.

It is my honor to be her eldest daughter. I am inspired by her courage. It is with great love and thanksgiving that I tell her story now.

I hope to live my life with the same hope and grace, no matter the challenges I face.

As you dare to face the challenges before you, let the stories here inspire you, just as my mother inspired me.

Dancing Slippers

Annie Marie's Story

I was seven when my mother died of tuberculosis. I had three brothers, an older sister, and a father with a broken heart. My sister had dreamed of becoming a teacher, but she put her books away to raise the family. My only dream at that time, at least as far as I remember now, was to learn to sew.

I was fascinated with fabric, threads, and sewing machines, and I did my best to learn to sew and contribute to the household by making simple clothes and mending worn garments. Times were tough for our little family. We lived on a farm near a small Texas town, and we grew and raised every bit of food we ate. We lived with few luxuries, but we had the essentials.

Then, my father died as a result of a simple infection in his neck. Today's antibiotics might have saved his life. But, that was then.

The children were farmed out to various relatives, and I became a servant in my uncle's household, the extra child in an already full family. But, I had my sewing and one other ability—I played the piano. No one had taught me. I had learned to play by ear in church.

I loved music and dancing all the way down to the tips of my toes. I made my own dresses so that I could go out dancing at the Saturday evening church socials, my reward for a week's hard work. It was there that I danced into the arms of my future husband, Marvin Huss.

Our first child, Marv, suffered greatly from asthma. The doctors warned that he would not live through childhood if I did not take him out of the damp climate of the South. In spite of my fear of leaving our small town, my husband and I took our son across the country by train to begin a new life in the big city of Los Angeles. There, I raised my young son, working as a seamstress during the war.

And there, Marvin and I danced! We danced in all the famous ballrooms from Hollywood to Santa Monica. We always plopped our young son on a chair at the sidelines and twirled away, never worrying for a moment about his safety. That was then.

My daughter, Linda, was born 10 years after Marv, and I devoted myself to raising both of them the best way I knew how. Raising my children was the best time in my life.

My dreams have never been big dreams, but they have been important dreams to me: to raise my children as good citizens, to support my husband, to keep a clean and orderly home, to be a good neighbor, and to conquer my fears.

After the death of my Marvin and 65 years of marriage, my heart actually stopped beating. Doctors revived me physically, but I had to restore myself emotionally. With a stent in my heart, I talked myself back into life.

Only a few years later, I was challenged again with the passing of my dear daughter, Linda. Countless times, I said, "I can't understand why I'm still here when Marvin and Linda are gone." Once again, I eventually overcame my grief and carried on. Now I hear myself saying, "I must be here for a reason. There must be some good I am supposed to do." My will has carried me through.

I have wrinkles on my face now, but they don't worry me. Since I am 96 years young, they are to be expected. They all disappear when I smile. I do that often.

Should you find yourself in the Albertson's supermarket in La Quinta, California on a Thursday morning, you just might see me. I am the woman in the brightly-colored pants and tops jetting down the aisles, gathering my groceries to take back to my apartment where I live happily by myself. You might notice that I am wearing dancing slippers.

California Dreamin'

Dolly's Story

Retirement. What a sweet word to me as I labored endlessly in the library of a small Midwest city for many years. Every day, I dreamed of moving to California and enjoying the palm trees, the warmer weather, and having family close by for the rest of my life. Finally, I turned 65 and received my long-awaited pension. A new life awaited me—"California here I come!"

What excitement I felt as I packed for my new home—until I collapsed to the floor. Unable to move, I lay on the floor waiting for help to come. Seven hours later, my son arrived home from work and called 911.

I had suffered a stroke. A large blood clot in the cerebellum of my brain impaired my motor and verbal skills. I was in intensive care for over a week. I could not walk, talk, write, or hold any food down. The doctors wanted to put a feeding tube in my stomach, but my sisters rushed in and said, "Absolutely not." For some time afterwards, my sisters fed me—food, love, and support—and they prayed that their sister would come back. Eventually, I was transferred from intensive care to a hospital room and later to a rehabilitation center.

I made slow, steady progress. I worked hard during hours and hours of physical, occupational, and speech therapy. I learned how to walk, how to pinch a clothespin, and how to think of the rights words to make a sentence. I did not give up.

As time passed, my sisters insisted over and over again that my dream of moving to California was still possible. Slowly, I began to believe it too.

On November 15, five months after my stroke and in a wheelchair, I moved to California. My sisters were with me every step of the way. I have continued my therapies and have recovered much of what the stroke took away.

With a loving caregiver nearby and support from family and friends, I often bask in the view from my back porch: the ocean, the palm trees, the California sun. Sometimes, my neighbors sing to me: "Hello, Dolly! It's so nice to have you back where you belong . . . ." In my heart, I dance.

The Other Side of Fear

Jan Fraser

I have experienced many terrible things in my life and 98% never happened.

MARK TWAIN

Most of us know all too well what Mark Twain was talking about. We build up fear around whatever step we need to take to live our dreams, and it freezes us solid. It limits us and prevents us from experiencing the dream work that we know will sail our souls and spirits to new heights.

Fear can hold us back from seizing the moment and stepping into that dream.

Years ago, my self-esteem was in the basement. I had just gone through a divorce and was not in a good place. I felt ugly. I looked at myself and said, "What can I do to make myself feel more attractive?"

Whenever I looked in the mirror, all I could see was a large nose on my face. I hid it as best I could with my long hair, and yet, there it undeniably was every time I looked at myself. I began to dream that I could change it.

No doubt about it, I was fearful. What would it look like? Would my daughters recognize me? Would I recognize me? Would I be sorry and want my old nose back even though that would be impossible?

Nevertheless, after my mother watched Phyllis Diller on TV, I made an appointment with Phyllis Diller's plastic surgeon (no kidding), Dr. Franklin Ashley of Beverly Hills, California. My mother had called me up after the show was over and said, "Jan, you only have one face. You need to go to the best." So I did.

When I arrived at Dr. Ashley's office, I recognized famous people in the waiting room—all hiding behind sunglasses—and I thought, You are out of your league here, Jan. Fear hit me in the stomach and told me that I did not deserve to be there. I wasn't enough.

I talked myself into staying and went in to meet Phyllis Diller's surgeon. He was a kind, soft-spoken, giant of a man who asked me why I was there. Working to find my voice and fighting my fear, I said, "I would like a new nose."

Without skipping a beat, he replied, "Yep, I can make it smaller, straighter, and shorter. I think you'll like it." He said that after the operation people would ask what I had done to look so good. My new nose would look so natural, he assured me, that no one would have a clue that I had changed it. That sounded beyond fantastic, but there was another bigger issue.

I told him I was a single, divorced mother of two daughters, and I had little to no money to pay for this nose change. Somehow, I worked up the courage to add that I worked for a doctor, and since Dr. Ashley was a doctor, would he consider a professional courtesy discount? Dr. Ashley shocked me by saying that he would do my surgery for the miniscule fee of $200. I started to cry and thanked this man I had never met before for being the kindest person on the planet.

To say I was afraid on surgery day would be putting it mildly. However, I pushed past my anxiety and envisioned not hiding my nose behind hairstyles and never being teased again. The operation was a success.

It was the single most positive step I have taken in my life to boost my self-esteem.

Some people have told me I was vain to have cosmetic surgery. I think it was a positive step toward my dream. Fear comes in many forms, and sometimes we fear that others will judge us and reject us.

"Oh, what the heck, go for it anyway," I learned at Jack Canfield's training. And go for it I did.

Each day, as I look in the mirror to put on my makeup, I realize once again that facing your fears and daring to make changes can be the best catalyst to getting your dreaming started. The next time you are feeling that paralyzing fear, know that there must be something really big and wonderful around the corner for you.

Dare to conquer your anxiety and fear. Dream of positive changes in your life. Dance in delight when you are on the other side of fear.

Courage is being scared to death and saddling up anyway.

JOHN WAYNE

Chapter 2
Coming to Terms

To see things as
they are, may just
be the wisest way
to see things.

© Sally Huss

Our lives improve only when we take chances, and the first and most difficult risk we can take is to be honest with ourselves.

LILLIAN CARTER

Facing the Music

Jan Fraser

Coming to terms with who you are is a crucial part of dream building and happiness. For many women, this involves facing difficult and painful issues within themselves and in their lives.

Facing the music is never easy, but the dance on the other side is magnificent.

In this chapter, some of the authors of *Dream Dare Dance!* share their own deeply personal life experiences with you in the hope that you too will face the most difficult obstacles before you. If these kinds of issues are also preventing you from living your dreams, set yourself on the path to getting them handled.

Dare to come to terms. Dream of the life that is possible on the other side of this journey.

Let the stories in this chapter inspire you to do what you need to do to live the life of your dreams.

Things do not change, we change.

HENRY DAVID THOREAU

14 Days in Detox

Joanne Proctor

There are over 15 million alcohol-abusing people in the United States at this time (2009). One-third of them are women. I was one of them.

This fact was beginning to sink in as I wandered around the first floor of a detox center just after I checked myself in. Women in their mid-forties, men of all ages, young women, and even teenagers were lounging about, dressed in everything from jeans and t-shirts to pajamas, house coats, and slippers. No one seemed to notice that I was a patient, since I was cleverly tending to the other patients' needs so that I could appear to be one of the staff. Coffee, tea, juice, iced cloths to wipe their brows, warm blankets to comfort their bodies—whatever I could do to help. It was what I did best.

I am a professional counselor and caregiver.

Within a couple of hours, I knew the stories of everyone in the room, except for a couple of holdouts. There were people from all walks of life—housewives, businessmen, construction workers, civil servants, students, and musicians—but their stories all had the same unhappy ending. Mine did too, but at that moment I wasn't sharing. I had just arrived, and I was maintaining my image of the "competent counselor" which I had mastered over years of covering up my addiction.

One of the rules for getting into this detox center is that you have to be clean for 24 hours before you check in. Like everything else, these rules did not apply to me. My head began to pound as the numbing effects of the drugs and alcohol I had ingested just prior to entering detox began to wear off.

The next day, the law of cause and effect hit me hard as years of consuming alcohol and sedatives abruptly stopped. Every bone in my body ached and daggers ripped through my head. Withdrawal set in, dissolving my competent counselor self-image and exposing the truth—I was a wrecked, abused, middle-aged woman.

Like most alcoholics, I had never considered myself one. I was neither dirty nor incoherent, and I never staggered. I was a responsible citizen. I worked in social services, raised a family, paid my bills, and was a good neighbor. I contributed. I even helped others solve their problems and lead more meaningful lives.

But underneath this façade of normalcy, alcohol and pills had taken over. My addiction had grown. I lived only for opportunities to drink and that took me straight to the bottom.

My history is not an uncommon one—an alcoholic family, my mother's death when I was a child, an unstable and abusive father, partying teenage years, drunken boyfriends, a bad marriage, and divorce.

What saved me was something that was terribly right in my life—my two beautiful daughters. My hope, my goal, my dream—what I ached for most—was to be a better mother. As a bonus, I wanted to stop hiding behind a mask. I longed to feel happy rather than hopeless. These are the reasons I took the steps necessary to change. I checked into the detox center of my own volition.

I was in the detox center for only 14 days, but in that time, I learned a lot. Perhaps most importantly, I learned that only two out of three people who enter a detox program are successful and never come back. I was determined to be one of the two. My life depended upon it. I had finally learned that, at any time, I am only one drink away from being drunk. It was difficult to imagine my life without alcohol, but I knew I could never drink again.

With hard work, I have been clean and sober for 21 years.

My heart dances as I think about what I have accomplished in my life and what lies ahead. My feet skip as I play with my grandchildren whom I may never have known. And, I thank God everyday that I dreamed of a different life and dared to do something about it.

Once you choose hope,
anything's possible.

CHRISTOPHER REEVE

Healing a Broken Heart

Lila Larson

After 17 years of marriage, my husband and I adopted a beautiful baby boy. We named him John. We raised him with as much love and care as we possibly could, delighting in him and supporting him every step of the way. Our biggest dream was to have a close, loving relationship with our son.

Twenty-two years later, near the end of July, the phone rang in the middle of the night. I feared it was the night intensive-care nurse at the hospital where my husband was recuperating from a heart attack. A familiar voice said, "Hi Mom, I'm in the hospital and I'll be in here for four months under 24-7 lockdown. Will you come visit me?" I hadn't seen or heard from our son in 18 months.

My son was a drug addict, but I didn't know it yet.

Seven years earlier, John had moved away from home to an apartment, and over time, our visits had become more and more rare. Weeks and months would go by when we did not hear from him and could not reach him. A few times, he had agreed to meet me for lunch or coffee. But the visits had been brief, and he always had asked for money.

As the years passed, his body had deteriorated. He had become pencil thin with black circles under his eyes. He frequently had "spaced out" while we were together. I had suspected that he was making choices I didn't agree with, but I could not imagine exactly what he had been doing that made him this way. My love was blind.

Then, he completely disappeared from us.

We had seen him at Christmas time. But after that, we did not hear from him, and we could not find him. As winter turned to spring, and spring gave way to summer, and fall and then winter returned, I drove through the streets of the city at all hours of the day and night, trying to catch a glimpse of my son or spot one of his friends who might be able to offer even the tiniest clue to where he might be.

The private detective we spoke to about how we could find John said this: "I can find him for you. But I can't make him come back to your house or make him contact you. He knows where you live and he knows how to reach you if he wants to. My best advice is to live your own life."

I ached for my son, but I stopped trying to find him. It was 18 months after that Christmas that he called from the hospital.

I found John quarantined in the isolation ward. His chest X-rays had showed two golf-ball-sized holes in his lungs filled with TB bacteria. How could this have happened?

While I sat beside John's bed wearing a gown, a mask, and gloves, I discovered the truth—my son was a drug addict. High on drugs, he had often partied for days at a time with other users in a closed space—an apartment, a motel room, an abandoned room. All a person with untreated TB had to do was sneeze to infect John.

How could I have missed what was happening? How could I have been so utterly blind? My mind raced as I stroked my son's ravaged face, held his bony fingers, and tried to cool the fever raging in his frail body. Now I knew for sure why he had not shown up for family dinners, birthday celebrations, Thanksgiving, or Christmas. Now I knew how I had lost him, or at least, what I had lost him to.

As I listened, a whirlpool of emotions battled in my heart, but I bit my tongue, preventing myself from uttering judgments or scolds or advice. That was not what he needed.

At the same time, my thoughts flew to my husband who was laying across town in yet a different hospital. His recent heart attack had been severe, and to make matters worse, when he had arrived in the emergency room, a medication designed to break up arterial clots had caused a stroke. After he had been moved to ICU, a nurse called a "Code 99" and asked me to leave the unit. My husband's heart had stopped. He survived, and a stent was placed in his arteries. As John lay in the isolation ward, my husband was recuperating—across town.

I felt that my family was shattering. How could I manage? What should I do? I would care for both of them the best I knew how.

Each day, I rose early and gardened for an hour to ground myself before visiting hours started. I returned phone calls from loving family and friends. I visited my husband for several hours before driving across the city to visit with my son.

I prayed for strength.

My husband was sent home 10 days after his heart attack with the prescription to take it easy, that is, avoid raising both hands over his head, avoid lifting heavy objects, lie with his ankles uncrossed, and rest. My daily visits to the isolation ward to visit John were followed by taking my husband to a cardiologist, a wellness center for cardiac rehab, a general practitioner, and a rheumatologist. My husband was angry and struggled to adjust to his new lifestyle, especially because his independence was so curtailed and he could not return to work. Somehow, we managed.

During the four months that John was in the hospital, I spent many hours talking with him about life, decisions, consequences, and his plans for the future. My heart was full of new hope that he would make different choices after he was released. We celebrated his 23rd birthday with a large chocolate cake and 23 candles.

John broke contact with us within one week of being released from the hospital and settling into his new apartment. Our phone calls were not returned. Letters and cards went unanswered. Months passed. Christmas came and went. I packed up his Christmas presents and put them in the attic for him to open another day. Father's Day went by. Birthdays. My husband and I grieved differently. I cried and withdrew. He was angry and showed it. We struggled to create a life of our own, limping along on separate paths. Family and friends joined in a prayer chain of love and support for our beloved son.

After seven months had passed without any word, one day the family of John's roommate called to ask if we could pick up our son's belongings—they needed to rent the room to someone else. I sorted and packed what my son had accumulated over the last seven months. What had he done here? Where was he now? Was he breathing? My heart was so heavy I could barely cart the boxes to storage, carry the bags to the garbage, and scour the room. Never have I felt such heartbreak and fatigue. Yet, I knew that I had done all that I could to love and support him. He was making his choices, and those choices did not include contact with us.

Over time, I have come to realize that John gave me many gifts while he was in the isolation ward. He asked me to come and see him. We spent time together. We shared our thoughts and memories. We celebrated his birthday together. I was able to see the happy, loving son he had been years ago, his body and spirit free. He was still there beneath the ravages of his drug addiction, sickness, and anguish. I am certain that he knows that we love him regardless of the choices he makes. I know that he loves us.

Now, I have to allow him to continue on the journey he is choosing once again. I can only pray and wait. I have learned that it is his choice to get healthy, to live a safe lifestyle, and to become the person he was born to be. That has become my dream.

My prayers are that each day he will choose health and a safer lifestyle and that he will return to us one day whole, healthy, and ready to pursue his dreams. I trust the goodness in his soul, and I choose to believe that he will return to us.

Broken dreams do show up in our lives. It's what we choose to do with them that prepare us to be whole in heart and to dream, dare, and dance again.

Two years and three months after writing my story for this book, John came back to us. He entered Teen Challenge, a global Christian rehabilitation program, where he remained for a year. He rediscovered his values, created new habits, learned about a clean and sober lifestyle, and developed a network of new friends who are clean and sober.

John has been clean and sober for one year and six months at this writing. Each day continues to be a blessing for all of us.

Only I can change my life.
No one can do it for me.

CAROL BURNETT

The Blank Stare

Sue Savage

*H*ave you ever felt like you've fallen through a hole into pitch darkness? Or experienced such sadness that you do not want to get out of bed even though nothing in your life has changed? Do you sometimes feel there is no conceivable way out or up? I have.

At times, I have no desire to do anything, have no intention of getting out of bed, and simply lie there and obsess about everything I dislike about myself. Sometimes, I feel like I am in the center of the spokes of a wheel, and no matter which way I turn, there is no escape. It is as if an invisible thief has trampled me, robbed my energy and joy, and now holds me hostage. All that's left is an empty shell that only resembles me. I do not recognize myself.

Looking in the mirror, I can see the blank stare of depression.

I experienced my first bout of depression in 1979, when I was a senior in college. Thirty years ago, there were no TV commercials for anti-depressants, no screenings at women's health fairs, and no one even remotely famous bravely coming forward to share his or her life story. Most of us who knew depression's relentless grip suffered in silence, too ashamed to seek help. My plan? Hide it.

After I graduated, I took a college teaching job, and I went about my work and life simply hoping no one would notice when my depression hit. Yet, try as I might, my closest friends always detected my withdrawal. At first, they jokingly called these my "black days" and kindly endured my silence and sadness.

However, during my third year of teaching, one brave, dear friend pulled me aside, confessed her own battle with depression, and described the treatments she had received at the campus mental health center. Off I went, relieved that I was not alone and hopeful that perhaps there was help out there.

I peppered my first counselor with questions: Why do I feel like this? What have I done to cause this? Is it treatable? Will it end? I learned that if I was going to realize any of my hopes and plans—if I was to enjoy life at all—I would have to dare to learn to face, manage, and live with my depression and whatever was behind it.

My counselor suggested a two-pronged treatment: anti-depressants and therapy. One required enduring possible unpleasant side effects, and the other required the courage to wrench out painful experiences buried over the years.

Was I ready for this? I wasn't sure. What I did know was that I could not live like this much longer—it had become unbearable.

I started treatment.

After experimenting for months, I finally found the right anti-depressant. My spirits lifted, although to this day, I still wish that my body chemistry could be adjusted without medication.

Over time, my goal in therapy became to find my inner voice—the voice that had gone underground. The voice that had relied on speaking from my intellect to get me through life. The voice that lay underneath all that I had repressed. The voice that trembled as I started to try to express my own needs and speak up for my true self. The voice that was silenced by my own family. This all required yanking out and facing all of my experiences and emotions— the good and the bad. I forced myself to feel it all. I learned that in order to alleviate the depression and to experience true happiness, this was simply what I had to do. It was not easy.

Even so, I discovered beauty there. And truth. I found that certain truths only reside in that darkness. As it is said, "The truth will set you free."

I began to experience true and honest joy.

Eventually, armed with my anti-depressants and the tools I acquired through working with my gifted counselor, I left therapy. I got married, had a son, and went to work at a local community college.

Many successful semesters of teaching English came and went. The longer I taught, the more papers I received from students who were contemplating suicide, ready to quit school, or asking my advice about a relationship. I felt at such a loss to help these kids explore their issues that I decided to return to school for a master's degree in counseling.

During my counseling internship, I found my passion. I fell in love with helping other people heal, and not long afterward, I joined the staff, specializing in treating women with depression. I believe that my own personal experience with depression has given me great compassion and a deep understanding of my clients. To those who come to me for help, I hope that I am able to pass on all that I have learned from my own experiences and all that my own loving, gifted healers have given to me.

Depression can be an all-consuming, dark, and frightening place to be. Although I still have bouts of depression, they do not cripple me as they once did. I know now that depression does not need to interfere with your ability to realize your dreams.

Please, do not suffer in silence. Life really is worth living.

Growth itself contains
the germ of happiness.

PEARL BUCK

Let The Change Begin

We cannot change the world we see,
Till change begins in you and me,
We change the world around us when,
The change begins within.
Let the change begin,
Let the change begin,
Let the change begin within.

. . .

The lesson from the willow tree,
Is strength in flexibility,
When nothing seems to go my way,
It's time to learn to sway.

. . .

Patiently,
Courageously,
Be the change you wish to see.
Let the change begin,
Let the change begin,
Let the change begin within.

LYRICS BY JANA STANFIELD AND MEGON MCDONOUGH

Chapter 3
Health

Health likes to be
appreciated while it's
here and not wait
until it's gone.

© Sally Huss

Dreaming of Health

Sue Savage

What does good health mean to you? Is your health something you've always taken good care of or something you've taken more for granted? Is it something you struggle with?

What does your dream state of health look like? Are there dares you need to take to achieve it?

Whatever your health today, every woman over 40 has lived through a revolution in health care. We are privileged to live longer and with a higher quality of life than ever before. We need not only dream of long, healthy lives. We have the arsenal to take decisive action.

How reassuring to know that when we see our middle years as a major transition, we have the privilege of knowing that we will live 30 years or more after turning 50.

Dream a dream of a healthy life. Dare to take the action you need to accomplish this dream. Dance each step, each breath, of the way.

Change is the constant, the signal for rebirth, the egg of the phoenix.

CAROL BURNETT

Time for The Change

Jan Fraser

*P*icture this: I was speaking on customer service to a large group of professional men and women from Verizon when disaster struck—and not in the form of rain or snow. It was a natural heat wave aimed right at my chest and midsection. I was on fire and experiencing my first hot flash.

I didn't know what was happening at first: A major heartburn attack from my lunch of everything-on-it pizza? Someone turned off the air conditioning? The possibility that the dreaded, mysterious menopause had finally struck never occurred to me. All I knew was that I wanted to rip off my turtleneck and cool down. Proper etiquette for speaking at a conference ruled out that option.

Later, I had to laugh when I remembered my speaking topic that day was "Putting Out the Fire in Your Unhappy Customers."

Since my first hot flash was intense but short-lived, I thought that was the end of it. After all, I was "young," despite my 50 years. It was not to be. Life became a volley of hot flashes by day and "sweats" by night in the weeks and months that followed.

When I realized I needed to do some research on the subject, I consulted my *Webster's Collegiate Dictionary* that had accompanied me to college in 1965. The *Webster's* definition of menopause: "The period of irregular menstrual cycles prior to the final cessation of the menses, occurring normally between the ages of 45 and 50."

At least, I was on schedule and not going to miss the train.

At the same time, the *Webster's* definition was downright depressing.

Who wants to be "irregular" or in the "final cessation" or "ceasing" of anything? Especially something that made you feel young and vibrant? As much as I had feared and dreaded the day when full-blown menopause and all its wonderful symptoms would hit my life, I feared what it meant to my aging process even more.

It meant that I was on my way to being an older woman and my youth was over. At least to me.

Menopause was a subject that never came up between my mom and me.

I asked her about dating, kissing, and how to keep a boy's hands to himself. My mom even accompanied me to that eighth-grade maturation movie about how babies are made. She answered all my questions. When I was older, she talked to me about my honeymoon, and what to expect in the bedroom. There was no talk whatsoever about midlife menopause.

My mom was a nurse, and her advice and knowledge were invaluable about childbirth, how to bathe and take good care of my babies, and how to cook a turkey.

But there was never talk of menopause.

I'm sure she was going through it herself. However, it was the "silent passage" as Gail Sheehy described it in her ground-breaking article in the October 1991 issue of *Vanity Fair* and later elaborated on in her book, *Silent Passage— Menopause.* We did not talk about it, and we were not the only ones. Menopause had long been a subject women rarely speak about and certainly not above a whisper or openly in any book.

Today, menopause is more openly talked about—on the stage, in countless books, on TV—and may be coming soon to a theater near you. We have made progress, but we have a long way to go.

For one thing, "senior summer," "a simmer moment," and "a personal summer," all euphemisms for menopause, do not come near to describing the heat that comes over you like a furnace blast at the most unpredictable, and often, unwanted times—meetings, dinners, weddings, standing at a cashier, talking to your boss, and of course, giving a speech.

I plan to share the message of menopause with my daughters so they'll be more prepared. I am going to call it menopause. Call a spade a spade.

When I was 43, I secured a peach of a job as a flight attendant, trainer, and speaker for American Airlines. At my new job, I met Karyn, a woman who had traveled all over the world as an international flight attendant for American for 25 years and was then the supervisor of the "Image Team" at American for all the new-hire flight attendants. We were the same age and became fast friends.

While Karyn and I worked side by side every day, we had numerous talks about everything under the sun, including "The Change," as we called it then. We decided that we simply would not let menopause happen to our bodies. "The Change" was not about to "change" us. We were not going to allow it to propel our beloved bodies into "old age," strip us of our youth and vigor—or happen to us at all. We planted our feet in concrete and said, "It will not happen to us."

Well, I'm here to tell you that I couldn't stop it. Menopause did come, and it stayed with me for a few years. I *think* I'm on the other side now.

But I'm only guessing. That's one of the trickiest parts about menopause—there are no firm parameters. You never really know when it will start, what your symptoms will be, or when you'll be done. Starting menopause is a step into the unknown.

It can be mysterious and frustrating—unless you come to terms with it, learn about it, and see what this new stage of life can offer. When I started to see it this way, menopause became a marvelous time in my life.

"The Change" changed me. And I like the changes.

Menopause is a time to dream and to dare to make changes in our lives.

Many of the women I know have made revolutionary changes in their lives once they hit menopause—walking away from a marriage, starting a new career, joining the Peace Corps, running marathons for the first time. To this day, I do not know if it is because hormone levels have such a profound effect on our emotions and how we see the world, or whether the onset of menopause often makes us acutely aware of how many years we may have left. Probably both.

Either way, an amazing thing often happens during menopause.

What is important to us can suddenly become crystal, startlingly clear. With astounding clarity, many women stand up and say, "I simply don't have time for this any more. I want this for my life now."

Menopause offers a gift—an unusual ability and opportunity to examine your life, dream of what it can be, and go for it.

Menopause is a time for dreaming, daring, and dancing.

There's no doubt that it can be hard to dream and dare—let alone dance—when you feel like you are in the middle of the Sahara in a raging sandstorm without a compass. I think I could've navigated my way through the storm of menopause a bit sooner if I had known more.

This is what I wish I had known about menopause—this is what my mother did not tell me:

Life with little or no estrogen and progesterone is different.

Hormones are powerful stuff—powerful enough to allow us to bear children. Low hormone levels can cause insomnia, dizziness, skin changes, irritability, difficulty concentrating, extreme mood changes, bloating, hair loss, weight gain, muscle pain, and joint pain. At least. Sound fun?

And how about the slowing down of our metabolism to a slow crawl? Notice your midsection expanding? Now maybe you know why.

Then there's "perimenopause." Whose mother ever told them about that? To be fair, she probably didn't know about it either.

So, in case you don't know, perimenopause is the beginning stage of menopause in which you start experiencing the effects of low hormone levels, but you are still ovulating. "George" is still visiting, as my college roommate used to call it, and George may visit once a month or he may visit only sporadically. You are not technically in menopause until George has not visited for one year. By then, you're glad he's gone.

Because fluctuation in hormone levels can be like a roller coaster. When once you may have had PMS once a month, now PMS symptoms—and often a much stronger version of them—can hit at any time, on any day. Weeping, irritability, and depression can come on you like wildfire, and then disappear just as quickly.

I have known women who started perimenopause and menopause in their 30s, 40s, and 50s. Most of them had no idea what was happening to them as their emotions whipped around like a hurricane. Changing hormone levels can have a *profound* effect on your emotions.

Although I am not a physician, I do know that some call progesterone the "well-being hormone." Its presence promotes a sense of well-being. Without it, or with much less of it, you can feel depressed, hopeless, and wildly irritable.

If you're lucky enough to have had no symptoms during your own perimenopause or menopause, I am genuinely happy for you. I toast your good fortune. But if you are experiencing symptoms—physical or emotional—it is helpful to know as much as you can so you can do something about it. Knowledge can help you find your way. It can enable you to take concrete steps to manage your symptoms.

Menopause does not have to be a roller coaster ride. It can be one of the best times in your life.

It may be time for others to bear the children. But it's not time for sensible shoes.

However, it might be time to wear cotton more often—in layers so you can strip when a hot flash hits—shower more often, and sleep with a fan. One friend of mine carries a portable fan wherever she goes.

You can avoid common hot-flash triggers like spicy foods, hot drinks, alcohol, and caffeine. You can do yoga, learn to mediate, and exercise often to reduce stress which can increase symptoms.

Some women find relief with hormone replacement therapy and are staying on it. Others are successful with anti-depressants.

It is important to find what works for you.

Consult your doctor—she can determine your hormone levels and recommend strategies to reduce symptoms.

Read as much as you can—know and understand what is happening to you. It is your body and your life. It matters. It is important to journey through this time of life with knowledge and a doctor or mentor you trust.

I am not an expert. This is not the whole story. This is only what I know.

This is what I wish my mother had told me.

I am here to tell you that I have experienced menopause, and I am, in fact, older now. But, I don't feel "old." I still feel young and vibrant and as alive as I ever did. I have changed. My body has changed, my outlook has changed, and I have changed my life. I like the changes. I believe I am wiser now. I am a woman, and I accept and celebrate all the phases of my womanhood.

Dream your dreams. See the new life that menopause is opening up for you.

Dare to accept and take charge of the changes in your body. Dare to dream and change your life.

Dance with me as we celebrate our womanhood—in all its beauty and all its phases.

Our lives are not over. They have, indeed, only changed.

What the caterpillar calls the end of the world, the master calls a butterfly.

RICHARD BACH

Heart Sounds

Sue Savage

*B*eing the idealist that I am, I never doubted for one minute that my healthy lifestyle would protect me from any major health issues. I voraciously read the latest health information, exercised daily, and had every preventive screening possible. When I imagined my old age, I saw myself as energetic, self-sufficient, and eating a piece of cake from a chocolate cake with 100 candles. Then, I had a heart attack. I was 51.

It was a crisp October morning. Brilliant yellow leaves sailed to the ground as I relished my usual early morning run, got in my car, and started off down the road on my errands. And then, I fainted. I am told that my car drifted into the left lane, went up over the curb, tore down a fence, and crashed through the side of my neighbor's garage. The next thing I remember is climbing into the

ambulance. The emergency room doctor diagnosed what had happened—
Me—healthy, fit, vibrant Sue—had suffered a heart attack.

I was admitted to the hospital. Two weeks and many tests later, my team of
doctors concluded that I had experienced "sudden death syndrome." Basi-
cally, the heart's electrical system goes haywire, causing you to faint or drop
dead. My doctors recommended implanting a cardiac defibrillator in my chest.
One of the doctors held up the defibrillator—it was the size of a cell phone.

I was scared, to say the least. I no longer felt in control of my life or my body.
How did this happen? I asked myself over and over. Why, after all the rigorous
dietary and fitness measures I had taken for years, did my body betray me?
My thoughts and feelings swept around like storm winds. Fear, then anger,
then calm—a vicious, tortured circle.

I told my doctors to weave the defibrillator wires into my heart. Even so, over
the next three months, my condition worsened, and I lived in and out of the
hospital. Eventually, when two liters of water had settled around my heart and
water was spilling into the surrounding tissues, I was placed in intensive care,
on the edge of death.

For the first time in 50 years, I was face-to-face with the harsh reality of my
own mortality. Would I live to see my 15-year-old son, Zach, graduate from
high school? Would I know his children? Would I die before my own mother?

I wanted to be well. I wanted my heart back.

I knew I had to dare to find the personal resolve to stay alive.

Suddenly, I could not ignore my real needs, which I had so easily hidden behind the daily business of my life. I could not pretend anymore. I could not profess things were okay when people asked how I was doing nor put aside my own needs for the needs of someone else. I had to learn how to express how I felt and what I needed to my friends, my family, my doctors, and myself. I had to take off my mask. My life depended on it. Allowing myself to be exposed and transparent—to express my own needs—was one of the greatest challenges I have faced.

A close, loving friend, whose greatest strength is emotional honesty, helped me more than I can measure on this journey. She was there for me 24-7. Before and after the surgeries, she was by my side. She crawled into bed with me and held me close when I was shaking with fear. She talked me through visualizations until I could find the peace to sleep. Our emotional honesty was unlike any human connection I had ever experienced. Each time I returned to my life outside the hospital, I yearned for this same intimacy and became committed to transforming all of my relationships.

Each time I take off my shirt, I can see the defibrillator protruding above my breast. At first, it instantly reminded me of everything I had been through, so this new addition was difficult to embrace. A gifted healer helped me to befriend it, teaching me to see that this is what my body now needs to live. I have created an image in my mind of my heart reshaping so it can hold truths about my life it couldn't previously contain. By reframing my thoughts, I have come to forgive my body for betraying me. I now believe that, if I had not been in such good shape prior to my heart attack, I may not have walked away from the car that day.

While there are still days when I grieve, longing for the life of my old heart, I now pay closer attention to who I really am, who I choose to "dance" with, and refuse to "dance" to rhythms that don't feel right to me. My new truths allow me to dance forward. My gratitude for my second chance at life, its gift of transformation, and all those blessed people who have helped me on this journey, is immeasurable.

My dream, still, is to be eating chocolate cake on my 100th birthday. As I close my eyes, take a deep breath, and blow out 100 candles, my wishes will overflow from my healed heart.

I shall not die of a cold.
I shall die of having lived.

WILA CATHER

Defeating Breast Cancer

Jan Fraser

I remember when the first tiny lump was discovered in my mother's breast. Afterwards, she underwent a biopsy at the Mayo Clinic in Minnesota, and I called my father to see how it went.

"It's gone," Dad said. "They took the whole breast."

Only a tiny spec of cancer had been found in my mother's breast, but in those days, the treatment for any amount of breast cancer was a radical mastectomy. Her breast, along with the lymph nodes and muscle nearby, were all removed.

One day, following a difficult but successful recovery, my mother asked me to help her select a prosthesis for her breast. We met at a cancer specialty shop. I stared at the myriad of rubbery breast forms in the room while a kind saleswoman spoke in hushed tones to my mother about exactly what she was looking for. "A natural look," I heard my mother say. "Not too hot, I have hot flashes."

I followed my mother into a tiny dressing room, and we waited for her breast.

I was a young mother in my 20s. I was nursing. Perhaps this is why my mother had yet to show me her scars. Or perhaps it is because she knew how I'd react. I stared unabashedly when my mother undressed. It shocked me and it scared me. My mother—my best friend, my rock, the most upbeat person I have ever known, my dear, dear mom—was fragile and scarred. Once again, I was reminded of how tenuous her life actually was.

My mother hugged me as I started to cry. "Shouldn't I be hugging you?" I mumbled. And then, we wept together. As she nestled into my own milk-filled breast, I heard my mother say, "I just want to dance at Jennie's wedding reception." Jennie is my daughter. At the time, she was a toddler. We looked at each other, sharing the knowledge that neither of us knew whether this would come to pass but knowing that we were determined to try. I said, "Mom, I'm so happy you're here. That's all that matters." "No," she insisted. "I want to see Jennie in her wedding dress."

Breast cancer developed in my mother's other breast just a few years later. A modified mastectomy removed the cancer.

Years and years later, Jennie was married on a bluff overlooking the blue Pacific. Afterwards, we danced into the wee hours of the morning as the band played on and on and on. I thought of that day in the dressing room many times that night, as I gazed at my mother, who was dancing the night away.

My mother had defeated breast cancer and she was living her dream.

Hope is a waking dream.

ARISTOTLE

Early Detection

Mary's Story

*D*o you look like someone who might be diagnosed with breast cancer? Of course not. No one looks like they will have cancer. It just happens. And it happens to very good people—like me.

My message is short and to the point: If you haven't had a mammogram, schedule one *now*. Early detection saved my life.

Three years ago, my husband gave me an "executive physical" at Johns Hopkins Medical Center as an early 50th birthday present. Both of us are life-long fitness fanatics, and we were having a "turning 50" competition. My husband set the bar high with his physical, and now it was my turn to show him how fit I was!

My first appointment of the day was for a digital mammogram in the Avon

Breast Center at Johns Hopkins. I was not concerned at all. I had done my mammogram every year for the last seven years, and I wasn't due for my annual "squeeze" for at least another month. I was healthy, and there was no history of breast cancer in my family.

By the end of the day, I had undergone a digital mammogram, an ultrasound, a core biopsy, and I was scheduled for an excisional biopsy. My mind was spinning. How could this be happening to me?

Most women at this point ask themselves: If I have cancer, who is going to take care of my family? And that was my question. All I wanted to do was get that cancer out of me. I had a mastectomy a week later.

Fortunately, my breast cancer was diagnosed at an early stage. In my case, the digital mammography made all the difference because it can see through dense tissue (like mine) much better than an analog machine. What a brilliant machine! It saved my life.

Today, I am a three-year survivor, and I am proud to be associated with many brave women who have survived breast cancer. My hope is that my story will spur you on to get your mammogram, have your annual breast exam, and do self-exams regularly. No excuses. What you don't know *can* hurt you. I benefited from early detection, and I hope you will too.

My professional ballet slippers are back on tight now, and I continue to share my dance of life with my daughters and my world of women.

The Beauty in Healing

Annabelle's Story

When I was diagnosed with breast cancer in 2001, I began a journey towards wellness that radically transformed my understanding of life. My healing has included both conventional and alternative treatments, and the process has not always been an easy one. Yet, I have learned that disease is an opportunity to create a journey to healing, self-discovery, and self-care. It is not a journey bigger than you.

I was blessed to be living a wonderful life with my three beautiful children when suddenly my life changed directions. Like so many women, I found a lump in my breast and did not know what to do. Stricken by panic, fear, and shame, I immediately went to see my family doctor, knowing deep down that cancer was my destiny. I found the lump exactly one year after my father—the most important person in my life—passed away in 2001.

The cancer in my breast was removed, and my doctor recommended radiation and chemotherapy. I turned down chemotherapy.

Perhaps it was partly my fear of hospitals that initiated that decision. I had spent many days and nights with members of my family in their final hours. My mother had passed away when I was just seven years old. She was so beautiful and so young, just 45 years old. Somehow, throughout my life, I knew that there must be ways to heal the body—ways that did not save my mother.

From that first decision to decline chemotherapy, my priority was to find out every bit of information I could to heal my body. I tried to look at all aspects of health and healing, including nutrition, exercise, and alternative healing practices. It took a very long time, but I finally met a doctor who was willing to join me on my unconventional journey toward optimum health and wellness. We explored detoxification, dental amalgams, nutrition, meditation, exercise, supplements, and psychotherapy. Resolving past issues, learning to live in the moment, and opening my heart have been central to my healing. It has been a journey that gives me the good health I am fortunate to enjoy today.

I surrendered to my healing journey with all my heart and took every leap and dare available to me so I could enjoy the dance called life. I now know that there are many ways to heal. My own path to healing has included resolving past issues, learning to trust and live in the moment, and opening my heart. I am thriving and dancing today.

It is my deep feeling of gratitude for my experiences with cancer that inspire me in my current life purpose. I have written a little pink book, *Messages from the Heart: Learning to Love Cancer,* for anyone touched by cancer. It is a book filled with hope and resources for those looking for healing. In addition, I have started a non-profit organization dedicated to raising awareness about complementary cancer care. Please join me at www.learningtolovecancer.com. Everyone is welcome.

I have discovered the beauty in healing. I hope you will too. Blessings to you.

Dance for Health

Sue Savage

What a different life we are privileged to live today than the lives of our mothers and grandmothers because women's health issues finally have been brought out in the open.

No more whispering about starting your period, hiding a pregnancy under floppy clothing, or going through menopause on your own. Thanks to Oprah and many others, we can talk more openly about how our lives are affected by depression, weight, breast cancer, aging, and other health issues women deal with every day.

At last, women's health research is gaining long overdue funding and attention. Our daughters and granddaughters will be stronger and healthier as a result.

It is cause for celebration. Dance with me as I celebrate our fortunate and glorious lives.

Aging is not lost youth
but a new stage
of opportunity and strength.

BETTY FRIEDAN

You're in Charge

Jan Fraser

*H*ave you arrived at your present age miraculously, without much attention to how your body is treated and cared for? Many of us feel we need to do more to support our health and longevity.

The biggest challenge for many women seems to be exercise. It is not always easy to get motivated, but it is crucial. Think of it this way: If someone would promise to give you a million dollars if you exercised by 5:00 P.M. today, would you exercise by 5:00? I believe you would. Reward yourself when you exercise. Give yourself the equivalent of that million dollar motivational check to give your program a jump-start.

Maintain a healthy diet. It matters. Find one that works for you and stick with it.

Take care of yourself. If you've been under tremendous stress, take a few hours off and have that massage, pedicure, or some other form of sensual relaxation. Yoga and meditation both promote relaxation and longevity. If you take daily medication, do not get derailed by your busy life and remember to take it on time every day. It's easy to forget and not so easy to recover.

Feel good about yourself and do not compare your body to the latest top model or any one else. Only you have traveled your exact road to this point in time in your life. Don't accept and internalize any negative comments from other people about how you look. Try the "Mirror Exercise" described in "Lovin' the Body You're In" (Part One, Chapter 1). Look and feel the best you can for you.

It is your body and your life, and only you are in charge of it.

You are one of a kind. One in a million. Celebrate that!

The longer I live the more beautiful life becomes.

FRANK LLOYD WRIGHT

Birthdays

Jan Fraser

Birthdays are milestones—every one of them—so, celebrate them! You are alive—you have lived to be 40, 48, 56, 83, 102! Dance with joy for the life you have lived and the life before you. The best year of your life is now.

Choose a memorable place to be on your decade and half-decade birthdays. These birthdays are extra special, no doubt about it. Do something you will remember. Take a picture of yourself. Celebrate!

When I turned the big "Five-O," I was standing in front of Old Faithful, the geyser at Yellowstone National Park. Every time I look at that picture, it makes me feel full of energy and hope. I feel resilient—as capable as Old Faithful of continually erupting with enormous energy, force, and life. I am reminded that my life is a process of renewal. I am rejuvenated.

I hope you too dance on every single one of your birthdays.

Cheers to a new year and
another chance to get it right.

OPRAH WINFREY

Chapter 4
Juggling Acts

When one has little,
one is grateful
for anything. When
one has a lot, one
must be grateful
for everything.

Yes, there is Nirvannah; it is in leading your sheep to a green pasture, and in putting your child to sleep, and in writing the last line of your poem.

KAHLIL GIBRAN

Balancing Your Life

Teresa's Story

"Mom, can you pick me up after school today? We have music practice." "Mom, can you take me and Ben snowboarding?" "Mom, where's my socks?" Teresa, can you watch the kids? I have a meeting at seven tonight, and I forgot to put it on the calendar." "Mrs. Huggins, can you volunteer at the fundraiser?"

When requests for my time and focus pour in, a flurry of decisions needs to be made in one moment: Do I stop writing now? Do I bring my computer with me to the lodge at the ski area? Do I take my daughter to her friends, pick up my son and his friends, grab something quick to eat, and wake up early in the morning to complete my writing? What do I do?

Meeting the needs of the people in your life is a balancing act. Meeting those needs—and your own needs—is one of the greatest challenges women face.

Do you feel like you need to put your dreams on hold to ensure your family needs are met? Do you ever seem to get less sleep in order to accomplish all you desire in life? Do you ever wonder how much laundry can be accumulated in one week, only to remember the field hockey and lacrosse uniforms are covered in mud and need to be washed by the time school starts?! Life is simply amazing at times. How do all the dishes get washed, the clothes cleaned, the meals made, and the work accomplished? How do you get your kids to games and practices and friends and school events while coordinating family meals and time to simply be with your kids and talk? How do you find time to have a conversation with your partner uninterrupted by "Hey, Mom. . ."?

So often, women give up their dreams while supporting others and one day wake up and say, "Who am I? What have I accomplished? Do I matter at all?" Keeping in touch with your own desires along the way is crucial. The juggling act of life is not just about others—you need to be one of the balls in the air. It is important to create systems that support your dreams while you support the dreams of those you love. Instead of playing the balancing game without you on the roster, it really is possible to honor your dreams, dare to create time just for you, and connect with other women who dance with your spirit.

In 1998, I was awarded a scholarship to attend a seminar in California. That week changed my life—and I almost had not gone at all. I had thought: How could I leave my children? Who would be able to take care of them? How could I do this and not miss them? What if they get sick? Questions swirled in my mind.

When I shared my dilemma with an older woman friend, she replied, "Do you want your daughter to grow up as a self-sacrificing woman?" I replied instantly: "No! I want her to be able to dream big dreams and become anything she wants to become." My friend said, "I didn't do that when my kids were younger and now I see my adult daughters doing the same thing—giving up their dreams. I invite you to consider this opportunity as a way of sharing the gift of your children more fully with your husband and their grandparents. Give yourself permission to dream bigger so that your own children can do the same."

Those few words were the beginning of a new life path from me: daring to dream again.

I followed my heart, traveled to the conference, and later discovered that not only had my family survived, they had thrived. The time my kids had shared with their grandparents while I was away remains in their hearts as a special time to this day.

What I realized is this: It is important for me to balance my own professional and personal needs with my family's needs. Now that I am better at this, we share the responsibilities of our daily life more, rather than Mom doing it all. Our family feels in balance, and it has created more joy in our family. By allowing myself to connect with and value my own inner core, by risking, daring, and discovering solutions so that all needs are met—including mine—I now understand that a family involves a give and take between *all* members of the family.

How do we do it? Organized lists, a family calendar displayed by the phone, and a commitment by each family member to contribute. Whether we are on the ski slopes, cheering at a field hockey game, touring my husband's latest construction project at Hamilton College, or listening to Mom speak at her local book signing, we now celebrate all our accomplishments, including Mom's.

As I write now, I hear the infamous call, "Mom, do you know where my . . . ?"

Time for my balancing act!

Balls in the Air

Jennie's Story

*A*s a mother of school-age children, I've got all sorts of balls in the air—conjuring up healthy meals, trying to raise happy kids, keeping my husband happy, being indispensable at work, enjoying life, exercising, and taking care of my aging parents. Many of us struggle with finding a balance in our busy lives. How do we do it all and keep a sense of balance in our lives?

Here's what I think:

I think that we have to focus on what we're doing right. We have to be flexible, forgive ourselves, and not beat ourselves up just because something didn't go exactly according to plan. It doesn't mean we failed or are a bad mother, wife, colleague, or employee. We simply need to get up the next day and try it again.

I think that sometimes life is not in balance, and that has to be okay. When we drop everything to help a child with an important homework project, or help a friend in need, or decide we just have to have a minute for yourself, it's okay. So, hop on your bike or watch a chick flick. You're still holding on to the ball that says: This is most important now.

I think that we often feel like we have to be everything to everyone. I often take too much on my shoulders, think I have to be in charge of everything, and then end up running around like a chicken with its head cut off. If I leave my hubby to help with homework, do the dishes, and spend the evening with the kids, I feel like I have to leave strict instructions because he doesn't do it like I would do it. Can't I let go? Wouldn't it be great to take some time for myself and not worry about whether he's going to do exactly what I would do? I think if we all gave up some of this control, we'd be a lot happier.

We've all been told a zillion times that we need to take time for ourselves, and I think that really does need to happen. I am a happier person and better to everyone else in my life when I do this. Maybe we all need to put time for ourselves on the family calendar.

I think it would help to make exercise a priority. My friend Susan has to be at the gym at 6 A.M. in order to get this time for herself. But after she exercises, she can tackle the day and give to her kids, therapy students, and everybody else who needs her—a whole lot better. I think we all should follow her lead.

I think that it's hard to keep our dreams in focus when our days are filled with work, kids, partners, and other commitments. Even if we drop our "dream ball" for a while, I think it's okay. I believe it's still there. We might have to set it down for a time, especially when the children are very young, but we can still keep our dream in front of us. I have a "vision board" near my computer that spells out my dream for me just in case I forget it.

I think it's okay to let one ball drop once in a while. If it's been a crazy night and dinner's never gonna make it to the table if you have to fix it, stop and grab a pizza. It's not health food, but it keeps the sanity, and our bodies will make it through.

I think that we have to ask for and accept help when we need it. We are not an island. We don't have to do it alone. When I find others who lift me up, especially mothers who have kids at the same stage as mine and are struggling with the same challenges, I gain strength from them. This buoys me up and helps keep me in balance. It can be tough to admit we can't do everything, but when we do, I think it's the first step on the road to a more balanced and calmer life.

I think that small and simple things that are regular reminders of the blessings and bliss in our lives can make a big difference to our peace of mind. A song or even a favorite saying on my computer screen can remind me of the good things in my life. When I feel good, it helps give me the patience and strength to juggle all I am so blessed to have.

Juggling all the balls in my life while making time for myself, keeping my sanity, and not losing myself and my dreams in the process, is challenging, no doubt. But the truth is, right now I am living one of my dreams. To be a mother and a loving wife is the stuff of my dreams. I wouldn't trade it for the world.

Simplicity

Jan Fraser

Simplicity is a powerful tool for promoting happiness and reaching goals. When you simplify your life, you can better focus on what is truly important.

Take a deep breath and celebrate you and your life. If your life is too complicated and is preventing your happiness, sit down with paper and pen and figure out which activities you can live without.

Years ago, I went on a wilderness experience for women and camped by myself for 48 hours of "solo time." The lessons I learned while I was by myself in the Sierras are useful. I experienced how happy I can be with only the bare necessities.

Make a list of the happiest times in your life. Identify the events that occurred during those times, writing down anything that comes to mind, including your emotions surrounding those events. Write as long and in a much detail as you can. Then, try to identify your needs that were met at those times. This will give you a better picture of the needs you need to satisfy for you to feel greater happiness.

Look at what you procrastinate doing. If it is important, could you do it now? Get it taken care of.

If you are having difficulty honoring promises, then it is time to look at those. Make fewer of them or promise less.

Start eliminating the physical clutter in your life by keeping a charity box handy whenever you clean up. If you don't need the stuff, give it away.

Choose simplicity. It is a road to happiness!

Bare Necessities

Rhonda's Story

I sold my home last summer and the completion of my new home has been delayed until spring. I am living in my daughter's spare bedroom. Most of my belongings are in storage, so I do not have my "stuff" around me. Essentially, I am living out of a suitcase.

At the same time, I am starting my own business. I am using my 25 years as a Montessori educator to help families organize their lives.

Starting my own business while living out of a suitcase? How crazy is that?

Well, it was pretty unsettling at first. But I have learned a few things:

* My stuff doesn't matter that much. I think I was married to my house, my desk, and my stuff. Now that I'm without it, I don't know why I was so attached to it.

✳ I'm adaptable, but I didn't know it before.

✳ I think differently without all my stuff. It has helped me think out of the box.

✳ I don't need much: food, shelter, clothing, transportation, and a life purpose.

Right now, my new work is my life purpose. I need little else.

Gratitude

Jan Fraser

To recognize and understand what is valuable to you, even if it is not per-fect—to be grateful for the tender mercies in your life—can allow you to experience joy. Gratitude allows you to accept and celebrate where you are in your life, where your life has taken you, what you have, who you are, and where you are going.

Gratitude allows you to dance.

Start a "gratitude journal" today. Celebrate five things you are thankful for and write them down before you to go to sleep tonight.

Be grateful for your tender mercies every night.

Chapter 5

Traveling Companions

People come and go.
Friends, family and
loved ones stay
wherever they go.

Companions

Jan Fraser

$\mathcal{W}$e treasure relationships, old and new, that support us unconditionally in our struggles as we grow and celebrate life. Stop and think about those who are traveling with you.

As you examine the path you are on, where you are now, and where you are going, you can create a new path which takes you toward the future you want.

Dig deep and identify what your life purpose is. Who will you choose to be happy with as you create your future?

Look for those who respect both you and the differences between you, instead of your loved ones competing with you. These years can be the time to reinvent yourself and create the life you really want. You can choose happiness and joy in your life.

Who will travel with you on this journey?

Healthy Relationships

Sue Savage

*I*n midlife, our relationships—with partners, family, friends, and others—often move to center stage and can not escape evaluation. We begin to ask ourselves defining questions: What is it I want from my relationships? How connected do I really feel to this person? How will I go about getting my needs met? What will it mean to me if I don't?

Midlife is full of defining moments. It is a natural time for evaluation and change. It is a time to seek healthy, fulfilling, and loving relationships.

I believe that we all long for human connection. It is who we are. Whether or not we're consciously aware of it, this desire is always awake, at the core of our inner being. We are born of and into relationship. We live in relationship. We seek to understand what it means to be in relationship. We move from relationship to relationship learning about ourselves and others as we go, piecing together our own definition of what it means to love and be loved.

Where are you now in your different relationships? What is your soul whispering to you in your most private moments? Are you contemplating moving into or out of a relationship with someone? Maybe you're in a relationship that should be substantially improved, but it hasn't. Maybe something feels deeply wrong. Perhaps you're in the process of ending a relationship or you're afraid to enter into another relationship because your last one was so hurtful.

Perhaps you still dream about being in a nurturing, giving, and stable relationship. And dream you should.

You deserve to be loved in a healthy relationship.

No matter where you've been, are, or dream to be, you're never too old to move toward having healthy, loving relationships.

It takes courage to act on that dream.

Healthy relationships start with yourself, arising from inside of you and moving outwardly toward others. The more you understand, develop, and live out of your healthy, authentic self, the more capable you will be to attract and interact in a healthy way with another healthy person. You must be healthy yourself in order to be in a healthy relationship. You must know your true self, be able to find and express your own, true voice, and invite—not fear—personal growth. These are the first steps in attaining healthy relationships in your life.

In an unhealthy relationship, the authentic self can become deeply buried. The heart shuts down from neglect and in self-protection. Yet, the cry of the authentic self can be heard from deep within the soul. Listen to that voice. Daring to understand who we are and what we need is crucial to our ability to assess our current relationships and develop and find healthier ones.

Upon inspection, many of us find that some of our relationships are failing, unhealthy, and even abusive. Daring to leave an unhealthy, painful relationship can be extremely daunting. It often requires the willingness to go through even more pain. We become caught between two strong and incompatible desires: the desire for real love and happiness, and the desire for comfort and security. It is a painful place to be, as the desire for the known and the unknown battle within us.

But, it is important to honor your authentic self and live out of your true identity in order to attain well-being and real love. If you know in your heart that this is not possible in your current relationship, it is time to dare to admit it and leave, despite what you might lose or the pain you and others might experience.

Being accepted and loved for who we really are often becomes paramount in midlife. It is often said in midlife: "Take me or leave me." When the answer is "Leave me," you must dare to do so.

New tools are often needed for this life-changing task. You may have to learn to set boundaries with spouses, partners, and children. You may need to physically separate yourself from your partner. Whatever challenges you face, build a support team—it is crucial to weathering the emotional roller coaster you are about to board. They are there for you at the bumps, twists, and turns— and those times you feel like throwing up. Your support team is there to constantly remind you that it is all worth it because you deserve to be loved.

As you take your new dance steps, remember—now that you are willing and able to live out of your true, authentic self, you will finally be able to dance. Fill up your dance card and dance the night away.

Relationship Signs

Sue Savage

*D*are to dream of healthy relationships in your life. Dare to evaluate the relationships you are in now. As you do, let these signs start your journey. Taking a good look is the first step toward reaching your dream.

Signs of a Healthy Relationship

* You trust one another.

* You bring out each other's best qualities.

* You respect each other's individuality and embrace your differences.

* You're each responsible for your own behavior and happiness.

* Needs are expressed, respected, and met.

* No one tries to control the other.

* You both find pleasure in giving and receiving.

* Talking to one another is open and spontaneous.

* You find time to play and laugh together.

* Mistakes are accepted and learned from.

* There is a willingness to take risks and be vulnerable with one another.

* You both welcome affection and closeness.

* There is a balance between closeness to and separation from each other.

* You love and take care of yourself while in the relationship.

Signs of an Unhealthy Relationship

* You are not allowed to communicate your needs.

* Your partner tries to humiliate or intimidate you.

* Your relationship includes intense arguing, rage, or dangerous behaviors.

* One partner controls the relationship.

* One partner dominates the other.

* Your partner uses mind games.

* Your partner uses guilt to manipulate or shame you.

* Your partner blames you for his or her problems.

* You feel pressured to change to meet your partner's standards.

* Your partner physically hurts you.

* You are forced to do things sexually.

* You lose sight of who you know you truly are.

* You feel stagnant, trapped, stuck, miserable, and hopeless.

Remember—you deserve to be in healthy, loving relationships.

Let the stories here inspire you to seek healthy relationships in your life.

We know not where our dreams
will take us, but we can probably
see quite clearly where
we'll go without them.

MARILYN GREY

Surviving Divorce

Jan Fraser

I never thought it would happen to me. I was the goody-two-shoes, the girl next door, the "least likely to be divorced" in the high school yearbook (no kidding). I always had a picture in my mind of my husband and me on our 50th wedding anniversary surrounded by our children and grandchildren.

Divorce changed my picture. Am I proud of it? No. Do I want to talk about it? No. Will I tell you about it here in the hopes that it will help you and someone you love? Yes.

In AA meetings, people bravely stand up and say things like, "My name is Jane and I am an alcoholic." Well, "My name is Jan and I am divorced."

Daring to Leave
I think the hardest part for me was admitting that I had failed. I like to get things right. I played the flute in the high school marching band and made sure

I was in the exact right formation on the football field on Friday nights while never missing a note. I was the honor student. I did not want to be the black sheep in the family—ever. I wanted to be perfect. By seeking a divorce—no matter who asked for it first, no matter what the reason—I felt that I had failed.

The question "What will people think?" tortured me. What will the family think of me? What will the neighbors think of me? What will anyone out there say about me? And for how long?

It took everything I had in me at the time to severe the marriage tie. However, the safety and happiness of my daughters came first. So, when I realized they were in jeopardy too, my decision was clear. I would make the same decision over and over again to protect us all from harm.

Emotional abuse is a form of torture. It is a slow and steady deadening of self-esteem. To be subjected daily to the derision and degradation of the spirit is a reason for divorce. Some women withstand this better than others. I got a divorce.

I have said to myself that life is too short to dread waking up each day to face the constant wearing down of our personality and self-esteem. I needed to remain strong for my daughters. It is difficult to remain strong when you are emotionally mistreated.

My divorce was a transforming life event that changed my adult life like I never thought possible on my wedding days. I am certain people talked about me; it is always a news item for awhile. Then, it passes and a new local rumor circulates and your break up will be relegated to the last page in the paper and not the first. Have patience, this too shall pass.

I was a Bad Picker

Recently, I was speaking at a women's conference in Reno, Nevada, and the topic of the day was "Learning to Let Go." The audience was supportive and enthusiastic. I think they saw me as a professional woman with a stylish suit and every hair in place, and they doubted that any rain had fallen in my life. I told the audience that I had been divorced and that I wasn't proud of it. When I shared some of the reasons I had pursued a divorce, one woman in the back of the room had a message for me: "Jan," she shouted. "You're a bad picker!" Everyone laughed. It made me laugh too.

Maybe it was as simple as that. I had chosen the wrong man for me. I was a bad picker. Later, when I thought about what that woman had said, I forgave myself for all the pain that choice had created in my life. If you are reading this chapter for yourself or a friend, take heart that you may be a bad picker too. It's not the worst thing in the world. It's just something that happened.

Dream

I had dreamed of a life of happiness, it's true. When I was a young girl, I dreamed I would be happy all of my days. When I married my first husband, I dreamed that we would be happy together until death do us part. That's not what happened. We were not happy, and in order to find happiness for myself and my daughters, I had to leave. Those early dreams of mine did not come true, but that has not stopped me from creating new dreams. I had to let those dreams go and come up with new ones. It is simply part of the journey I have taken.

The most amazing part of my divorce journey to me is that I am truly happy now. I have found the love of my life, my soul mate, and we were married a year ago on a beach in Bermuda. Even in my wildest dreams as a young girl and a young woman, I never dreamed of this kind of happiness. I did not even know what it was. I know now, and it is beyond my imaginings.

I accept my life path now. I can see that without that very path I would not have been led to where I am right now. I want to be where I am right now. I am grateful everyday for the joys and blessings in my life.

I have made decisions that were daring and difficult. I have had to recreate and reinvent my life. Through it all, I have continued to dream. It is what made it possible for me to survive and thrive through divorce.

Do not be afraid to dream even if your relationship is not a happy one, even in your darkest hour. Dare to dream about a relationship in which you are treated with respect and loved for who you are. That is what love is about.

You deserve to dance.

We must let go of the life we planned,
so as to accept the one
that is waiting for us.

JOSEPH CAMPBELL

Free at Last

Bertie's Story

*L*ike most women, when I entered into my relationship with my partner, I dreamed it would last forever. Nineteen years later, I told myself that enough was enough—I couldn't take the physical and mental abuse any longer. I'd been walking around on eggshells for most of our life together. My partner's behavior was so unpredictable that I felt like I was living under a sword attached to a hairline string—at any minute, the string could break and the sword would drop. My three sons were also living in harm's way.

One night, at 4:00 A.M., I woke up each of my sons and said, "I'm leaving. You can come with me or you can stay with your father." All three chose to come with me, and we left without a place to go. I felt like I had jumped off a high ledge without a safety net. I had no place to go. I did not know where our next meal was coming from. Even so, I knew in my heart I was doing the right thing. I was taking a huge risk in order to stop living a nightmare.

I drove around until school started the next morning, and then I dropped the kids off at school. A friend took us in that first night. For the next several days, we bounced around from one friend's house to another. Finally, my husband's brother, of all people, said we could stay with him until we could get on our feet.

Eventually, we managed to get our own apartment. We all got jobs, pitched in, and did whatever it took to make ends meet. We didn't have much, but we had each other. That was all we needed. We went through a lot of hard times, but through it all, I danced in my heart with joy. I was free at last.

My sons are all grown now and have successfully found their way in the world. I live alone by choice in the same apartment, and I enjoy its safety and quiet. I celebrate the faith that gave me the strength to do what I so needed to do for me and my boys. Even though my sons are now spread out across the country, we are still very close.

I know our love will last forever.

Starting Over

Sandy's Story

*M*y husband had recently died and I was grieving. At that time, my teen-age son and I were living in a small town in Pennsylvania where people were judged by the family they belonged to. I did not know how I was going to escape the town's labeling of some of my relatives based on their reputations. I felt trapped and stuck.

Eventually, a few of my close friends convinced me that a computer would open up a whole new world to me. I bought a computer reluctantly, but they were right—my world expanded. I began to chat online with people from around the world, and soon I felt more open, and free, and started dreaming again.

My dreams surprised me. I dreamed of starting over in a new life. I dreamed of finding love again.

Soon, I discovered an online dating service. Aware of the importance of cyber safety, I used guidelines when online with potential dates and when I met a few of them in person. My dates never knew where I lived, and I met them in public places. My sister was on phone alert when I was on any of these "blind" dates. She would know if there was a problem if I called and said, "How is Freckles?" Thankfully, I never had to use the "Freckles" phone alert.

I met John online. Over the course of a year, we communicated online and by phone every day. We became good friends and confidants.

Finally, I traveled to meet him in Vancouver, British Columbia. It was love! We had already learned a lifetime about each other over the past year, so our meeting face to face was easy and felt right. We decided to marry, and I left the life I knew in Pennsylvania and moved to Canada.

I now have my dream relationship with John. He is my lover and my friend.

In the middle years of my life, I had a dream. I took a dare. And now I am dancing with my true love.

Midlife Adoption

Lila Larson

Seventeen years into our marriage, my husband and I began to dream of adopting our first and only child. I was approaching 40. Could we? Should we? How would we? We had long discussions exploring our thoughts and feelings. What did we want to have happen? What did we not want to have happen? How could we avoid repeating situations we had observed in other families? How would we support each other as child rearing issues arose? Were we too far along in our lives? And, of course, could our two dogs handle it?

When we finally arrived at our decision to adopt we were over the moon. The day we brought our son home was one of the happiest days of my life.

That morning, we dressed at dawn and began our two-and-a-half hour drive to the city of Brandon. Never had an October day looked so bright. It had been three-and-a-half long years since we first applied to a local social service agency to become adoptive parents. The years were rife with home studies, interviews, couples' workshops—and the sheer agony of waiting.

Once in Brandon, we found the social services department in a government office building and opened the door to an office full of cubicles separated by five-foot walls. At the end of one aisle of cubicles, we could see a new baby dressed in yellow. I grasped my husband's hand. Could that be our son?

A smiling woman, a social worker, scurried toward us, checked we were the Larsons, and led us to a small conference room. "Please wait here," she said. She turned back, on her way to the door, and said, "Do you understand that if this baby is not the one you want, you can say no?" We stared at her, dumbfounded. "Your name will go back on the waiting list. There will be no penalty." I still could not find any words. "You do not have to accept this baby," she said. "Are we clear?" We somehow finally nodded and she left.

Alone in the room, we panicked. What could she possibly mean? Would we not be able to take our son home? How could we ever leave behind the baby we'd been waiting for so very long?

Moments later, the door of the conference room opened, and the woman stood in the doorway—holding our son. A smiling, blue-eyed baby boy. He was indeed the beautiful baby in the yellow clothing that we had seen upon our arrival. At seven-weeks-old, he already had dimples in his cheeks, elbows, and knees. His hands were big and his feet were long. He was going to be tall.

What joy as we held him, explored his tiny being, fed him a bottle, and changed him, passing him back and forth between us.

The woman returned within an hour. She looked at me as I held my son and said, "Are you sure that this is the right baby for you? You must be absolutely sure before you leave here." I clutched my baby tightly to my breast and stepped back from her. "We're sure," my husband said. "If you'd like," the woman said, "you can meet the birth mother before you go."

She was only 15 when she gave birth. We could only imagine the wrenching of her heart as she sat with us that morning. We shared tears and gratitude as she held her child, and our child, for the last time. We attempted to give thanks to the courageous young woman who had conceived, carried, and delivered our precious son. Her gift to us is without measure.

I do not recollect much of what was said or done after that. I know we dressed John in a new, blue bunting bag before we headed home.

Suddenly, it seemed, there we were, driving home with our new baby. We had dreamed for so very long of having a child, dared to endure the three-and-a-half years of rigorous preparation and waiting, and now here he was. Our beautiful baby boy lay snoozing in his car seat. We could not take our eyes off him. We could scarcely believe our eyes.

We were looking at our dream.

Wings of Eagles

Deep inside me, there's this longing
Like a bird that needs to fly
I've been captured by indecision
But I was born to sail the sky
I will fly on wings of eagles,
I will sail on wings of change
Unencumbered by the past,
I face the new day unafraid
Life is rich with possibility,
This is my moment
My time to shine
All it takes is a little faith
And on the wings of eagles I will fly
There's a stirring in my spirit
Telling me I'm free to fly
There's a small voice, I can hear it
Telling me it's time to try
I will fly on wings of eagles,
I will sail on wings of change
Unencumbered by the past,
I face the new day unafraid
I am ready to let go of
The fear that held me back
I am ready to spread my wings
And make a difference that will last
All it takes is a leap of faith
And on the wings of eagles I will fly

LYRICS BY JANA STANFIELD

Part Three

Dance

Dance as though no one
is watching you,
Love as though you have
never been hurt before,
Sing as though no one can hear you,
Live as though heaven is on earth.

ALFRED D. SOUZA

Chapter 1
Dancing Partners

Life is a dance.
Find a partner!

© Sally Huss

The Dance

Jan Fraser

*D*ancing is one thing all of us know how to do. From our earliest days on earth, we move to the music. Our style may get more refined as we grow taller, but the instinct is just the same—free-wheeling, joyous celebration. Some of us do "chair dancing" or "car dancing" when we have limited space. A good song comes on that we love the music to, and we dance and sing along. We dance with that free spirit that comes from inside. We feel it and it feels good.

Dancing is all good.

I used to dance as I cleaned my house. I listened to Rick Astley, The Supremes or John Denver. I could really get going! Think back to the times you've danced. Was it when a beautiful surprise landed at your doorstep? A call from a friend who was thinking about you? Flowers from an admirer? Or just because you're happy to be alive?

I knew a friend who sent flowers to herself anonymously. She was the only one in her office who knew she had sent them. The card simply read "From someone who loves you." I love that. Let's face it, we all need to love ourselves and celebrate for ourselves. This friend knew how to dance.

That is what the *Dance* is all about for all those who *Dream Dare Dance!* It is about celebration—celebrating who you are and what you've accomplished, big and small. The *Dance* is joyous celebration—on the dance floor, in your kitchen, or in your heart.

Create a celebration for yourself when you have dreamed the dream and dared to make it happen. It is your turn to dance.

Let's see you go for it!

You are beautiful and your dance is too!

Soul Mates

Jan Fraser

I dreamed about a choice relationship with a man for as long as I can remember.

I wanted intimacy on every level: a glorious-playful-passionate-heartfelt-physical love combined with mutual respect and a spiritual, intellectual, and emotional connection. I wanted a companion to experience life with. Someone who would understand my strengths and frailties and would love me, cherish me, and treat me like a lady through it all. In my dream, I would love him on all those levels too.

That's not too much to ask, is it?

After I turned 50, I hoped it wasn't too late for me.

I learned more about soul mates from a 30 "something" woman named Diane who I met on a plane en route to the U.S. sometime after my 50th birthday. As we talked about relationships (over airline peanuts), Diane defined the situation like this: "You can be married to a soul mate, a roommate, a help mate, or a cellmate." Well, no doubt about it, I was looking for my soul mate. Not my roommate. Not my cellmate. I've had a few of both to know the difference.

Diane went on to say that her husband is her soul mate. I was intrigued, as you can imagine. Diane described how in sync she and her husband are on most issues. If they aren't in sync, they listen to each other's views with mutual respect and make decisions based on what they've shared. She said being with her husband is a joy, even when sharing the smallest of activities.

As I listened to Diane, I thought: Wow! She found her soul mate at a young age and bravo for her! Twice her age, I hoped there was still a chance for me, although I worried it was no longer possible. Diane had read somewhere that the percentage of people who live with their soul mates is only 8-10%.

I wanted to be in that select group.

I was always the one running across the room to convince some man to love me, even if he wasn't looking my way. I would twist his arm so he would notice me and love me. At times, I changed myself like a chameleon to be whatever a man wanted so he would love me.

This kind of intense searching for a partner and changing to fit someone else's picture always led me to unhappiness, frustration, and divorce. Years of working the kinks out of a relationship was definitely not the way to find my soul mate. At some time or another, I came to realize that I was trying to push my square peg into a round hole, and the result would never create the soul mate connection.

Years went by, and I had no luck finding a soul mate. So, I stopped searching.

I was definitely *not* looking for a soul mate when I was collecting nametags at a conference in San Diego and noticed a man from a place where I would be speaking later that year. I said a simple hello, found out his name, and exchanged a few words.

From that simple beginning, our friendship grew into an altogether different relationship than I had experienced before. At first, I wasn't sure what was happening. I was completely baffled when he began to support the activities I was involved in. The lengths to which he went surprised me even more. One time, when I organized a team of women to walk 39 miles for breast cancer in Long Beach, California, he flew there to assist our crew. I thought: Whoa!

Why would this man fly more than 6,000 miles round trip to support our walk team? One of my girlfriends' response to this question was, "Jan, he's courting you . . . ." It was all new to me. But his kindness and generosity touched my heart. As months passed and we saw each other in different environments and events, I found myself caring deeply for him.

I had never felt this way about a man before. It was not only romantic love. It included deep respect and support for each other's goals and life purpose. It contained loving each other's children as our own. We wanted to be together because everything we did together was a joy.

In college, I read *The Prophet* by Kahlil Gibran. I didn't fully understand the section on love until now.

To wake at dawn with a winged heart
and give thanks for another day of loving;
To rest at the noon hour and meditate love's ecstasy;
To return home at eventide with gratitude;
And then to sleep with a prayer for the beloved
in your heart and a song of praise upon your lips.

I get it now. I am in midlife and in love with my soul mate.

Last year, we were married on a beach in Bermuda, where we share a home with the handsome teenage son I never had. My daughters, sons-in-law, and seven grandchildren celebrated the day with us. When I asked my new son if he thought this marriage was going to be good for his dad, he replied, "Yes, I can see he is happy and I am happy for him."

I may be a slow learner to some, and it may have taken me a bit longer to get here, yet my journey, however bumpy, has allowed me to value what I have now. I treasure every day we are together. My daring is done.

I now dream and dance on the beaches of Bermuda with my new and ever-lasting love—my soul mate.

Let the stories here inspire you to seek out loving relationships in your life.

Treasure the love you receive above all.
It will survive long after your gold
and good health have vanished.

OG MANDINO

Once in a Lifetime
Elaine's Story

I married Melvin. That started a 43-year love affair with the man who would become the man of my dreams.

I wasn't sure he was the man of my dreams before I married him. I was a young 19-year-old. He kissed me and I went all mushy inside. But it scared me to think of being married.

We became life partners and soul mates. We had three daughters and worked together in business. We enjoyed laughter, companionship, travel, and an intense love connection.

He was taken from me by lung cancer 15 years ago. I miss him every hour of every day. I have my daughters and grandchildren to enjoy. I work at a local yarn shop and knit all the time. I give my knitted sweaters, purses, shawls, hats, and dresses to those I love. It keeps me busy. It keeps me focused on being here and not with Melvin.

Friends have encouraged me to meet men and go on dates. I am attractive, well-dressed, and funny. They don't understand that Melvin is the only man for me, and I am not interested in meeting anyone else. I can't do it.

I don't know why he was taken first. I ask myself that question all the time. I just know I am here. I know I must not be done yet, and that gives me hope, thinking I will somehow make a difference for my friends and family.

I dare myself to make each day count, as Melvin would have wanted me to do.

I inspire others to believe that a once-in-a-lifetime love is possible.

I smile and I dream.

Families

Marg's Story

My parents were hard-working and extremely frugal people. Father always had a large pot of soup on the stove so that whoever dropped in would be fed. Mother sewed my clothes, creating works of art for my personal and professional wardrobes. I loved working with her as we discussed what was needed for different events, and I always felt like a queen in one of Mother's creations.

From both of my parents, I learned the value of creating a home from whatever you have and sharing it with others. I learned the importance of family.

Early in my life, I decided nursing would be my own way of sharing with others. After I gained experience in a succession of supervisory positions in Canada, my native country, I decided to add to my education by pursuing graduate study in the United States. There were many lonely days and nights for me while I was away from home, and the letters I received from my friends and family helped me stay focused and connected.

For many years, my career continued to keep me far from my family. After completing my graduate degree in nursing, I accepted a position in Red Deer, Canada, where I saw the need for a nursing career advancement system. I went on to design, develop, and implement this plan in the province of Alberta, and it was later used throughout Canada.

My parents eventually followed me to Alberta, and we shared a home there while I taught at the University of Alberta in Edmonton. It was an absolute delight to be living again with family, and the value of their love and support is immeasurable. As time went on, I became the President of the Canadian Nurses Association and developed systems and processes for the betterment of all Canadian registered nurses. I was thrilled to see my career progress, but once again, it took me away from my family. When I was offered a position as the dean of nursing at the University of Calgary, I moved to Calgary.

My family was miles away again, and my circle of friends and colleagues became my family. I loved the camaraderie with the women I coached, mentored, and counseled. I entertained and had great fun holding gatherings with the diverse mix of people at the university. I have grown as an individual and a professional with the support of all my "families."

What I have learned is that family can exist in many forms. We each have nuclear and extended families as well as our family of friends. There are also other groups we may be a part of—professional colleagues, music lovers, ballet attendees, art lovers—all of whom we spend time with for specific activities and periods of time. These are our families too.

As I look back on my 80-plus years, I am thankful that I chose to stay close with my family and create family groups in my life. Even now, I share my experience and perspectives with my visitors, offering great listening as my gift to them. No one really pays attention to my aging limbs, slower walk, stiff hands, and special needs. They keep me vibrant, filling me in on what they are facing in the world.

I challenge you to choose to enjoy each day. Make it the best that you can. No matter what happens in your life, lessons can be learned and joy can be found.

Dreams can be pursued. Take the risk. Step forward. Dance!

Homecoming
Kathy's Story

When I was 15, I gave up my newborn son for adoption. After graduating from high school, I married the father of my son, and we had three beautiful girls. All those years, I never stopped thinking about my son. I felt a deep need to connect with him, as if a part of me was missing. My yearning and grief deepened with each passing year, especially as the joy of raising my daughters helped me better understand what losing a child really means. For 30 years, I dreamed of finding my son. I was willing to do whatever it took.

My husband did not share my need to find our son, and this, along with other issues, led to our divorce. My girls chose to stay with their father in our family home. I moved out and got a place of my own.

Less than a month later, my ex-husband called to say that our son was looking for me. Ecstatic, I danced and danced (and danced!) around my living room.

I discovered that my son's name is Vince. The first time we spoke, we stayed on the phone for hours—talking, laughing, and crying. I answered many questions he had carried inside of him for years, and he in turn answered mine. We shared our fear of being rejected by the other. We made a plan to meet at my home.

When the moment finally came to see my grown son for the first time and to embrace him, I felt blessed beyond words. I had held him in my heart for 30 years, but now I held him in my arms.

Eventually, Vince met his three sisters, and I met his adoptive mother and father. I am grateful to have been able to thank them both for loving and raising Vince—our son.

Since our initial homecoming, I have seen Vince take his marriage vows, and I now play with his two dear children. I continue to dance in my heart, just as I did in my living room when I first heard my son's voice on the phone that day.

Gifts given in love may come back to you. Mine did!

Halvsies

Marianne's Story

I met Marianne in a line at the San Antonio airport waiting for our Southwest Airlines flight. She was sitting on the floor reading a hardcover book, enjoying a moment of respite in a sea of airport stress. I didn't want to disturb her serenity, but when she looked up at me, we started to talk.

At first, I asked if she lived in San Antonio. She said she had moved to a small town near San Antonio some years ago and was heading to Chicago to visit family.

Her soft blue eyes mesmerized me as we spoke. She told me she lived in an amazing house on a creek and that the financial situation worked well for her and her friend, Merry, both retired women. "Everyone calls my friend "Bumpy," she said. I asked her to share her story with me.

She told me that she and Bumpy had known each other for 32 years as friends and colleagues in education. Now retired, they had created a win-win situation by sharing a home that they had custom built by a local builder.

"We each have a master bedroom and bath of our own, and we share the living room and kitchen," Marianne said. "Bumpy is the cook and I'm the cleaner. The kitchen has all the neat things built-in that Bumpy wanted, like lights in the pantry door when it opens. This way, we go halvsies on the house, utilities, and taxes. It works. We are happy there by the creek together."

Marianne had dreamed of finding an affordable living situation in a beautiful location with a caring friend, and there she was, living her dream. These two friends dared to jump into buying a lot on the creek, work with a builder, and finish their house despite the friends and family who thought it wouldn't work.

As I listened to Marianne's story, I was struck by how very many ways there are to dream, dare, and dance in your life.

We sat together, waiting for our flight, and I noticed the pink bracelet on Marianne's wrist. She proudly told me that she had been cancer free for three years. She plans to walk for breast cancer this year. I will be doing the same two-day walk. We will both be dancing for all that Marianne, and other women like her, have achieved in their dance of life.

Legacies

Lila Larson

*L*egacies come in all shapes and sizes: a treasured book, a china vase, a wedding dress, a lakeside cottage, college funds. The greatest legacy I ever received was from my grandmother.

I dream of leaving the same legacy to my own children and grandchildren.

It is a legacy of love.

Mentors

Jan Fraser

*B*e on the lookout for mentors in your life. As you journey on your dream path, the help and advice they can provide is priceless. Mentors come in all shapes, sizes, and places.

Professional mentors can teach you the ropes as well as deter you from heading down a wrong path.

Mothers can let you know when you are on or off course. If you're at the end of your rope or have given up on a dream, mothers can say just the thing that will get you back in the game.

Loving friends can provide a living example of what you hope to become, a kind of family you would like to create, or a way of life and purpose you would like to emulate.

Dream to find a mentor. Dare to look close and learn from them. Celebrate the part they have played in your life journey.

Angels Among Us

I was walking home from school on a cold winter's day
Took a shortcut through the woods and I lost my way
It was getting late, I was scared and alone
Then a kind old man took my hand and led me home
Mama couldn't see him, but he was standing there
And I knew in my heart, he was the answer to my prayer

Oh I believe there are angels among us
Sent down to us from somewhere up above
They come to you and me in our darkest hours
To show us how to live
Teach us how to give
And guide us with the light of love

When life held troubled times and had me down on my knees
There's always been someone to come along and comfort me
A kind word from a stranger, to lend a helping hand
A phone call from a friend just to say "I understand."
Ain't it kinda funny, at the dark end of the road
Someone lights the way with just a single ray of hope

. . .

They wear so many faces
Show up in the strangest places
To grace us with their mercies
In our time of need
Oh I believe there are angels among us
Sent down to us from somewhere up above

They come to you and me in our darkest hours
To show us how to live
Teach us how to give
And guide us with the light of love

LYRICS BY ALABAMA

Sisters Are the Mainstays

Jan Fraser

> Strong is what we make each other.
> MARGE PIERCY

I need my sisters. Every one of them.

Do you have a sister who you love? Have you created that same indelible bond with another woman in your life—a friend, a co-worker, a daughter, your mother? I hope you have. These women are your "sisters" too.

My mother, sisters, daughters, and friends are all my "sisters," and each of them blesses my life. The world wouldn't be the same without them and neither would I.

When you have to walk that lonesome valley by yourself, your "sisters" will be on the valley's rim, cheering you on, praying for you, pulling for you, intervening on your behalf, and waiting with open arms at the valley's end. Sometimes, they will even break the rules and walk beside you. Or come in and carry you out.

When each of us began this adventure called womanhood, none of us had any idea of the incredible joys or sorrows that lay ahead. Nor did we know how much we would need each other. Every day, we need each other still.

Sisters are our mainstays.

A sister is a gift to the heart, a friend to the spirit,
a golden thread to the meaning of life.
ISADORA JAMES

A young wife sat on a front porch on a hot, humid day, drinking iced tea and visiting with her mother. As they talked about life and marriage as well as the responsibilities of adulthood, the mother turned a clear, sober gaze upon her daughter.

"Don't forget your sisters," she said, swirling the tea leaves at the bottom of her glass. "No matter how much you love your husband, no matter how much you love the children you may have, you are still going to need sisters. They'll be more important to you as you get older. Remember to go places with them now and then. Do things with them. Stay close."

"And don't forget: 'sisters' also means your girlfriends, your daughters, and all your women relatives too. You'll need other women. Women always do."

The young woman thought: What a funny piece of advice! Didn't I just get married and join the world of couples? Surely my husband and the family we may start will be all I need to make my life worthwhile.

But as the years tumbled by, the daughter came to understand that her mother was right, of course. She kept in close contact with her sisters and nurtured her relationships with her daughters and her female friends. As time and nature worked their changes and their mysteries on her, all of her "sisters" became the mainstays of her life.

After almost 59 years of life, here is what I've learned:

Time passes.
Life happens.
Distance separates.
Children grow up.
Love waxes and wanes.
Hearts break.

Promises are kept or not.
Careers end.
Jobs come and go.
Parents die.
Colleagues forget favors.
Men don't call when they say they will.

But—

Sisters are there no matter how much time and distance are between you.

A sister is never farther away than you can reach.

Give to the world the best you have. And the best will come back to you.
MADELINE BRIDGES

I loved my neighbor, Pat, who lived around the cul-de-sac from me in Valencia, California. We were both young mothers with two children. We both had a toddler and a baby so we were both busy running after them every day. We had so much joy for life and our families, and we were close friends.

Pat called one morning crying into the phone. She said she needed a biopsy for Hodgkin's disease, which ran in her family. Pat asked me if I could do her an unbelievable favor. I said, "Name it, I'll be there." Pat then asked me if I would nurse Nathan while she had her biopsy. Nathan, who Pat called her "little man," had never had a bottle, and she could not take him with her to the test.

I was quiet for a split second as my thoughts raced. Well, yes, I thought, I did have milk—I was nursing my daughter, Debbie. Yet, Pat called Nathan her "barracuda" because he was teething and insatiable. I had only daughters, and their nursing styles did not at all resemble a barracuda. Would Nathan nurse from someone other than his mother? Could I do such a thing? Finally, after a whirlwind split second, I said, "Yes. Of course. We're sisters, Pat. I'd do anything for you."

Pat brought Nathan to my house early the next morning. She hugged and thanked me. She cried as she kissed Nathan goodbye and set off for her biopsy. That morning, I breast fed both Nathan and Debbie, alternating between the two hungry babies. All went well, and it was an amazing experience.

After the biopsy results, it was not Pat who called. It was her husband, Bill, and he was in tears. He said that the biopsy had come back positive for Hodgkin's and that Pat already "had herself dead and buried." Pat's doctor had told her that she would have to start radiation immediately, and because the radiation would harm her milk, she would have to stop nursing just as fast. Pat was grief-stricken on both counts.

I asked Bill to put Pat on the phone. When I heard the sadness in her voice, I told her that we were going to figure this out and get through it. She said, "I'll have to wean 'the little man' and that is killing me." I said, "We'll figure it out. Let me do a little research and I'll call you back." I knew that if she could nurse Nathan through the radiation treatments she could keep her spirits up and fight the disease.

After a lot of investigation, the La Leche League's advisory board in Chicago informed me that all the newest research showed that the radiation treatments do not harm breast milk. When I told Pat the news, I think she almost healed on the spot.

Why did I do all this? To me, it was the only thing a close friend, a "sister," could do. I simply put myself in my friend's shoes. I asked myself what I would want and need if it were me. Then, I gave what she needed.

Pat nursed Nathan through the radiation treatments, Nathan is now a healthy, happy young man, and Pat is cancer free. Even though neither Pat nor I live in our cul-de-sac any longer and we make our homes a world away from one another, we remain close. We are still "sisters."

Sisterhood and brotherhood is a condition people have to work at.
MAYA ANGELOU

Some of us lose connections with our friends and sisters over time. Hard feelings and misunderstandings can create scar tissue which needs to be removed in order to rekindle the love between "sisters."

If this is your situation, go to a quiet place, close your eyes, and go back to a time when there was no wound and no scar tissue. Can you remember that?

Can you picture it? Dare yourself to return to that time and feel the feeling you felt then.

While you are reaching way down inside yourself, take the next step—dare yourself to heal the "sister" connection. Make a call to her, write her a letter, or give her a hug. Tell her you never stopped caring for her and loving her. Take responsibility for whatever part you played in creating the wound and in keeping the distance between you.

None of these actions are easy to do. Daring to take the first step is the hardest. Keep the vision of love from the past in your mind and move forward. It is worth it.

How will this daring action benefit you, your sister, daughter, mother, or friend?

You will feel good about taking the "higher road," as my mentor, Jack Canfield, has said to me and his audiences on many occasions. The higher road leads to greater success, excellence, and love in your life. At some level, your "sister" will feel good about your attempt at re-connection too. She will know you care about her.

You also build your self-esteem when you dare yourself to take the "higher road." It takes courage, and courageous acts build belief and confidence in your own worth. You will arrive where you did not think you could go—mending broken relationships with your "sisters." Just like when we were children and mended the broken wings of tiny birds, we must now work to mend the broken hearts of our "sisters" who feel for some unknown or known reason that we don't care any more. In the process, yours will be mended too.

I think daring to embrace a "sister" follows the "platinum rule": Do unto others as they would like it done unto them. If you are a "sister" living that rule, then you are a magnet for other loving people who share your like values. Together, we can celebrate and dance.

Be good to your daughters, they choose your nursing home.
JAN FRASER

I have been blessed with two beautiful, amazing daughters with whom I am very close. Do you feel the same way about your daughters?

Although my daughters, Jennie and Debbie, are married and have young families of three children each, we all come to each other for advice and support. This bond has developed over 30 years of being there for each other. It is born of mutual respect.

I dreamed of having a close relationship with my daughters, and I dared and worked to make it happen. To this day, they know that if they need me, I am on a plane as soon as I can get to the airport. If you have been blessed with a daughter, I trust you know exactly what I am writing about and feel as I do about sharing your lives.

If your relationship with your daughter is on the "outs" right now, take the steps necessary to gain it back. A daughter is your "sister" no matter how young she is or how old you are. Dare yourself to support her no matter what.

I plan on being close with my daughters till the last moment possible. That is my dream.

Dances with sisters are the songs of love and support for our dreams.
JAN FRASER

Dancing is one of my favorite things to do in life. I don't think I do it enough. Do you?

Do you dance with a "sister" when she has achieved a dream? Do you dance when you have a "sister" who is supporting and loving you through your dreams? I hope so. I do.

I danced at the weddings of my sisters, Bonnie and Dolly.

I danced with my sister, Bonnie, when she had her first daughter and when she gave birth to the first grandson in our family in two generations.

I danced with my sister, Dolly, when she adopted a baby boy.

I danced with Bonnie when she recovered from falling two stories off a ladder while cleaning her gutters and broke her wrist.

I danced with Dolly when she recovered from hepatitis.

I danced with Bonnie for inspiring me to get over my paralyzing shyness and speak to audiences everywhere.

I danced with Bonnie when she made me yummy eggs in her Manhattan apartment after she left the comfort of the Midwest to move to the big city.

I dance with Bonnie because she makes me laugh.

I danced with my daughters at their weddings.

I dance when my daughters tell me they love me. I hope they dance when I tell them the same.

I danced with my mother as she beat breast cancer, heart disease, hip fractures, and a fractured elbow. I danced in memory of her blessed spirit when she finally succumbed to Alzheimer's disease.

I remember all those dances still.

Start your list today. Right now. List the dances that you have experienced with your sisters and friends, the times when you have come together in celebration, in person or in spirit.

If the list of dances doesn't come freely to your mind, perhaps you need to listen to the music of sisterhood a little more and jump in!

Sisters alone are unsinkable. Sisters together are unstoppable.

Dances with "sisters" are the mainstays of your life.

Chapter 2

Dance Steps

Keep dancing.
Life's music
never stops!

Every day brings a chance
for you to draw in a breath,
kick off your shoes, and dance.

OPRAH WINFREY

First Steps

Lila Larson

$\mathcal{H}$ere you are in the process of deciding how you want to live with passion in your own life. May these suggestions help you as you dream, dare, and dance.

1. Your job is to focus on who you are, what you want, and what is important to you—without regard to your age, economic position, or geography. As you focus on these essentials about yourself and your desires, the "how-to" will show up.

2. Make quiet time in a place that you find peaceful. Wherever this sacred spot is for you, go there often and allow the free flow of your thoughts and dreams.

3. Dream along with your quiet mind—without censuring yourself. This

"free-form roaming" allows you to feel and see what you want without disapproving voices extinguishing the fires within you. It allows you to dream.

4.   If sleep is the way you dream best, before drifting off, ask yourself the question you want answered. Immediately upon awakening and before you get up, write down what came to you in your sleep.

5.   Allow your ideas to "bubble up" like bubbles in a champagne glass. Buy yourself a bubble blower and bubble soap. Watch with delight as the bubbles form, float, and land. See the iridescence of the bubbles and know that you too have ideas floating within you. Set aside some time to "bubble up" when trying to figure things out. Some "bubbles" will show up and point to what you want to do next.

6.   As you become clear on your purpose, set a time frame for making a decision. Otherwise, you may be tempted to continue circling—gathering more information and never getting to a decision.

7.   Once you decide on your goal, taking action is the next step on your journey. Make a list of five things that will move you forward. Take one step each day, even if you are tired or busy. Each step forward will increase your confidence and open up new options for moving forward.

8.   Share your dream with those who want you to succeed. Their enthusiasm, support, and caring will provide you with a team of cheerleaders to bolster your journey and bounce ideas off of when you run into obstacles.

9.   As you move forward, make time to feel what you are experiencing. You can figure out what is and isn't working for you by allowing yourself to become clear about what you feel. Your path may need adjustment. Your feelings will lead your way.

10. Create opportunities for laughter and humor in your life. Laughing can

give us a new and more relaxed perspective about ourselves, especially when we are not sure what to do next or hit an obstacle. Ask someone to tell you a funny story, show you a cartoon, or bring over a funny movie. Buy a laugh track and allow yourself to belly laugh along with it. Let laughter fill your sails and enjoy the ride.

11. When you are more relaxed, ideas form and point in a direction you may not have seen before. Make time for exercise and deep breathing to reduce stress. Take a walk, breathing in through your nose and exhaling through your mouth. After a short walk, you will be filled with endorphins, have more energy, and the "stuff" that was immobilizing you will be cleared out.

12. Surrender to the sureness that the universe is working with you to create who you are and what you want. When you've already taken the action to move yourself forward, it is time to relax and enjoy the ride!

I love to dance.

LEANN WOMACK

Creating a Dream

Teresa Huggins

* Vision Statement. Write down your dream and read it every day. Think big! It's all possible.

* Commitment. Make an internal commitment to your vision. Repeat it daily.

* Vision Collage. Create a vision collage made up of pictures and words to generate the feelings that you desire to manifest your dream. Put it someplace you can see it often.

* Daily Affirmations. An affirmation is something we state to be true about ourselves, other people, or other things. Write down positive affirmations about yourself and your vision. Use index cards that will fit in your purse. Keep them with you. State them frequently throughout your day. By focusing on the positive and on your dreams, you can make them happen.

✻ Visualize Your Intentions. Before you get out of bed, clearly picture the type of day you want to create. Set your intentions for the day. .

✻ Reflect. Consider each area of your life— family, friends, career, exercise, health, wealth, service, spiritual. What goals do you have for each area? What are you doing on a daily basis to create these goals step by step?

✻ Surround Yourself With Positive People. If someone doubts you, think "Next!" in your mind. Be open to meeting someone who will support you.

✻ Refueling Time. Take time for you, even if it is only a few minutes a day. If you nurture yourself, you will have more to give others and your dreams.

✻ Gratitude Shower. As you shower, offer gratitude for the aspects of your life and the life ahead of you.

✻ Focus on your Essence. What state of being do you want to create in your life? When you are experiencing life with a state of joy and love, solutions come.

*I have enjoyed greatly
the second blooming*

*Suddenly you find—at the age
of 50 say—that a whole new life
has opened before you.*

—AGATHA CHRISTIE

Declare Your Dream

Jan Fraser

The first women's retreat I created was held in the Red Mountains in Utah. We spent our last night in front of a blazing fireplace talking about our dreams and goals to one another. Then, we shouted our dreams to the world.

One by one, each woman got up and declared her dream with her back to the fireplace. The fire warming her backside symbolized the fire lighting within her. Louder and louder each of us shouted, announcing our intentions, our plans, and our hopes. We shouted them out to the farthest corners of the park.

In that moment, each of us created an indelible print. We stamped our dream onto our internal planner. We were each on our way to our life purpose, empowered by speaking our hopes and dreams to one another and declaring them to the world.

We invite you to join with us on this dream path.

Speak your dream. Tell a friend or a loved one. Shout out your dream to the world.

Dreams Come True

May your dreams come true
If you want them to
If you're willing to do what it takes.
May we laugh and cry
And always try
To learn from our mistakes.
When we meet again
May we still be friends
And may your dreams come true.
If you want them to
If you're willing to do
What it takes.

LYRICS BY JANA STANFIELD AND AL MCCREE

Chapter 3

Dream, Dare, and Dance with us!

Dancing with the
feet is one thing.
Dancing with the
heart is another.

An Invitation to the Dream Club®

*g*et those dreams out of the drawers and bring them into the light. Dust off those cobwebs and open your heart and mind to new ideas, new possibilities, and new paths before you.

The party is just beginning! Shake a leg!

We invite you to participate with us across the United States, Canada, and the world by joining a local Dream Club! You too can *Dream Dare Dance* with us!

Dream Clubs are small groups of women meeting together to support one another to discover and actualize their dreams with the help of a facilitator to provide guidance and coaching. Dream Clubs meet in homes, schools, businesses, churches, synagogues, restaurants, or wherever you and your Dream Club feel comfortable and supported.

Find support for yourself and support others to achieve their dreams by joining a Dream Club. Magical things are sure to happen.

Now that you have read what other women have done, it's time to put your dancing shoes on. Get your dance card out. The floor is ready.

Please visit www.dreamdaredance.com to find the nearest club for you. If no club exists yet nearby, perhaps you will make that dream happen by creating one. We can help. Just send us an email at chapters@dreamdaredance.com or visit our website: **www.dreamdaredance.com**. We are creating one huge worldwide dance to celebrate our lives, our vitality, and our connection of love as we support each other to live the life of our dreams. We invite you to send us your story. Let us celebrate your journey to dreaming, daring, and dancing. Please send all stories to **info@dreamdaredance.com**.

We believe your dreams can come true.

Dream Dare Dance! with us!

Love,
Jan, Sally, Lila, Joanne and Sue

A Dream Dare Dance! Day

*C*reate a special day by bringing a *Dream Dare Dance!* event to your city. Learn how our team can help you create an inspirational *Dream Dare Dance!* event for you and your community of women while raising funds to donate to your local charity. Call Jan Fraser at 702-595-0900 or email jan@dreamdaredance.com for more details.

Or join us in Hamilton, Bermuda on October 3, 2009 for the world launch of *Dream Dare Dance!* Everyone is welcome!

Amazing Things

You will do amazing things,
With the choice each new day brings,
And with every step you take,
Bless the progress that you make,
The reason you live,
Is there in every gift you give,
Love your life, love your dreams,
You will do amazing things.

Amazing, Amazing,
You will do amazing things,
Amazing, Amazing,
You will do amazing things.
Oh, the places you will go,
And the people you will know,
Don't worry when or where or how,
You don't need to know that now,
You're on the right track,
No need to look ahead or back,
Just enjoy what this day brings,
You will do amazing things.

Amazing, Amazing,
You will do amazing things,
Amazing, Amazing,
You will do amazing things.

You don't have to work it out,
Just stay in the here and now,

Let your mind rest for a little while,
Sometimes deepest answers come,
When you're out there having fun,
So close your eyes, take a breath,
And smile.

Amazing, Amazing,
You will do amazing things,
Amazing, Amazing,
You will do amazing things.

JANA STANFIELD AND MEGON MCDONOUGH

The Dream Team

Jan Fraser—Keynote Speaker, Consultant, Coach and Trainer

Speaking to women around the world, I realize most of them want more joy, success, fulfillment, and love in their lives. My mission is to create life renewal for women who are looking to dust off their dreams and create new ones. I believe women are "unsinkable" and when united are "unstoppable." I can't wait to see how the world changes when we begin to *Dream Dare Dance!* together. **jan@dreamdaredance.com** **www.janfraser.com**

Sally Huss—Writer, Artist, and Former Tennis Champion

In my youth, my dream was to become a tennis champion. After competing at Wimbledon, I changed my goal. I became a fine artist, and I now create happy, free-spirited artwork for special products and special people. I hope your spirits are lifted by my art and musings as you read these stories and contemplate your own Dream Dare Dance! **sally@dreamdaredance.com** www.sallyhuss.com

Lila Larson—Life Coach and Teacher

As a life-long adult educator, my biggest joy has been in walking with my students as they dreamed, dared, and danced along their journeys. By contributing to this book, I continue to share in many more dreams. May this book bring you laughter, comfort, and joy as you choose a way of life that encompasses your dreams. **lila@dreamdaredance.com**

Joanne Proctor—Teacher and Healer

My life is about focusing on healthy and holistic practices. I am a Reiki master, trainer, and consultant. I have worked as a manager for over 20 years, and have formed two companies, Amber Woods Natural Care and Inside-Out Education and Training. I am dedicated to building self-esteem in women and encouraging better communication for a higher quality of life. I'm thrilled to be involved in Dream Dare Dance! **joanne@dreamdaredance.com**

Sue Savage—LCPC Counselor and Freelance Writer

As a professional counselor, I know that life is a journey as we go down our different paths. As we all worked together collecting stories to inspire women to dream, my own dreams emerged. Following my heart through some tough adventures, I'm more of a whole person now. It's my hope that as you are reading your own dreams will begin to surface too. I look forward to hearing how you dared to make your dreams come true and what that means for your life. **sue@dreamdaredance.com**

Contributors – Life Stories

We deeply thank all of the women who have shared their stories, lives, and messages with us. It has been inspirational beyond our expectations. Some of the women who contributed to *Dream Dare Dance!* would like to remain anonymous, and others would like to offer a way for you to reach them if you desire to do so. Here are those contacts:

Part One - Dream

Jin's Story: Jin Kyu Robertson: jkrobert@hanmail.net

Kate's Story: Kate Porter: www.crittercoalition.org

Katherine's Story: Katherine Bock: www.careertalentcoaching.com

Sam's Story: Margaret (Sam) Sansom: Central High School Foundation, 116 East Buena OVista, Barstow, California, 92311

Nina's Story: Nina McLemore: sales@ninamclemore.com

Maggie's Story: Maggie Dent: www.maggiedent.com

Deborah's Story: Deborah Lindholm: www.foundationforwomen.org

Sue's Story: Sue B. Wade: admin@walkinthetalk.org

Barbara's Story: Barbara Reid: bkreid@lifemax.net

Carol's Story: Carol Margolis: carol@smartwomentravelers.com

Getrude's Story: Getrude Matshe: www.bornonthecontinent.com

Kim's Story: Kim Mylls: www.boysbeforebusiness.com

Deb's Story: Dr. Deb Sandella: drdeb@innermagician.com

Peggy's Story: Peggy Cappy: www.peggycappy.com

Part Two - Dare
Annabelle's Story: Annabelle Bondar: annabelle@itsmeannabelle.com

Jennie's Story: Jennie Ritchie: jennie@simplespeakersolutions.com

Teresa's Story: Teresa Huggins: www.teresadhuggins.com

Rhonda's Story: Rhonda Munro: rhondamunro@gmail.com

Part Three- Dance
Joanne Proctor: *Dream Dare Dance* Original Song and Lyrics

Contributors –
Poems, Songs, Insights

We would like to thank all of our contributors. Their poems, songs, and words of insight are inspirational, and we are grateful. A very special thank you to:

Julie Anne Ford for "Dare to Dream." *Always Believe in Yourself and Your Dreams.* (Special Edition, A Collection from Blue Mountain Arts) Ed. Patricia Wayant. Boulder: Blue Mountain Arts, Inc., 1999.

Vicki Silvers for "Always Follow Your Dreams." *Always Believe in Yourself and Your Dreams.* (Special Edition, A Collection from Blue Mountain Arts) Ed. Patricia Wayant. Boulder: Blue Mountain Arts, Inc., 1999.

Jana Stanfield for "All the Good." Jana Stanfield, Jana StanTunes (ASCAP)

Janet Bray Attwood and Chris Attwood, *The PassionTest: the Effortless Path to Discovering your Destiny.* Fairfield: 1st World Publishing, 2006.

Thom Bishop and Ed Tossing for "Wake Up and Dream" lyrics. Performed by Jana Stanfield. Jana StanTunes/Eagle Woman Music (ASCAP).

Jana Stanfield and Megon McDonough for "Let the Change Begin" lyrics.

Never Let Go Of Hope

One day you will see that it all
has finally come together.

What you have always wished for
has finally come to be.

You will look back and laugh at what
has passed and you will ask yourself,
"How did I get through all of that?"

Just never let go of hope.

Just never quit dreaming.

And never let love
depart from your life.

JANCARL CAMPI